STRATEGIES FOR ADULT LITERACY AND ESL TUTORS

LITSTART

THIRD EDITION

D1451283

Patricia Frey
with ESL Applications by
Evey Renner

A publication of
Michigan Literacy, Inc.
1999

Library of Congress Catalog Card Number: 99-070706

Michigan Literacy, Inc.
2157 University Park Drive, Suite #4
Okemos, MI 48864

517-349-7511
Fax: 517-349-6667
e-mail: mli@voyager.net
http://www.MichiganLiteracy.org

Acknowledgments

Many thanks to:

Michigan Department of Education
Adult Extended Learning Services
for their support of literacy programs in Michigan

Library of Michigan
and the Library of Michigan Foundation
for their support of the literacy network in Michigan

New Readers Press,
a division of Laubach Literacy Action (LLA),
for assistance in the national distribution of LITSTART

Margaret Gawel and Larry Deck
for editing assistance

The hundreds of tutors, students, trainers,
literacy coordinators, administrators, family members,
libraries, organizations, and others
who have contributed their time, expertise, and support
to make literacy happen

The LITSTART Review Committee:
Donna DeButts, Marsha DeVergilio, Cindy Larson, Susan Ledy,
Lisa Pauls, Joy Rosynek, Jan Vern, Jean Villa, Cathryn Weiss,
and Levona Whitaker
for their invaluable observations and suggestions

Foreword

Michigan Literacy, Inc. is proud to present this third edition of LITSTART, representing the state of the art in adult literacy tutoring in Michigan.

Purpose

The purpose of this book is to provide you with the strategies and background necessary to tutor an adult in the skills of reading, writing, and speaking English.

History of LITSTART

LITSTART is the cumulative product of decades of tutoring, tutor training, program coordination, and research involving a network of thousands of people.

The first edition of LITSTART, written in 1986, integrated accepted adult teaching techniques with the concept of three tutoring levels. The second edition, published in 1990, introduced the strategy format, learning styles, content-writing instruction, a professional layout, a more holistic definition of reading, and many other improvements.

This third edition adds many new features, including:

- Addition and integration of English as a Second Language
- Enhanced guidance on the process of lesson planning
- Conversion of the Word Study chapter to the strategy format
- Guidelines on homework, grammar, portfolio assessment, and questioning techniques for checking comprehension
- Several new and revised strategies
- Elevation of the top level from fifth grade to seventh grade level
- Many other revisions and enhancements

We hope you find the book helpful and easy to use. As always, we welcome your comments and suggestions.

Levona Whitaker, Director
Michigan Literacy, Inc.

Contents

1

Tutoring Adults

*"Thank you for my tutor.
She is truly a gift from God."*

—Roberta, an adult student

Tutoring Adults

This chapter will provide you with an overview of the tutoring experience:

Welcome!

Welcome to the world of tutoring!

You are about to embark on an adventure that some tutors have found to be the among the most rewarding of their lives. Tutors often say that they gained from tutoring as much as their students did, not only in terms of new knowledge and skills, but also in terms of the satisfaction of seeing their efforts magnified into gifts of learning that made a real difference in someone's life.

That is not to say that tutoring is easy or magic. It is hard work, especially in the beginning; there are challenges to be met, questions to be researched, and ideas to be explored. But ultimately, it will pay off.

Your LITSTART book will provide guidance to help you find the best strategies and resources to make your student's personal goals a reality.

Enjoy your adventure with your student!

And thank you for caring.

The LITSTART Tutoring Experience

All good tutors in all subjects share such traits as patience, a positive attitude, and caring. If you have these traits, you can become a tutor. You can help someone learn to read and write or learn to speak English.

There are many ways to teach these basic communication skills. LITSTART encourages you to take a broad view, to explore the possibility that one student might flourish under one type of instruction and the next might do better with a different approach. A retiree who wants to improve his skills for enjoyment might need different instruction from a recent immigrant who wants to help her children in school.

You will have a choice of materials and activities.

As a LITSTART tutor, you will have a choice of materials and activities so that you can, over time and with the help of your student, assemble the best combination of activities for your particular tutoring situation.

These choices will make the tutoring experience more challenging than if you have a set formula to follow, but the choices will also open the door for you to develop exciting and effective lessons that match your student's individual needs, thereby maximizing your student's chances for success.

This book will:

- Help you identify your student's goals and learning style.

- Provide you with a variety of tutoring strategies.

- Offer guidance on how to choose the best strategies and materials for your particular student.

- Help you develop a lesson plan based on your student's personal needs and goals.

Your Mission

Regardless of whether you tutor someone who is learning to read and write or someone who is learning to speak English, your mission is the same:

> Your mission is to help your student pursue his or her personal goals by improving your student's ability to understand, speak, read, and write basic English.

If your student has a basic-skill goal, such as learning how to write checks or how to read to a child, your work is done when the goal is achieved (unless you can inspire your student to pursue a new goal).

However, if your student has a higher-skill goal, such as becoming an electrician or passing the GED Test, then your mission is to help your student prepare for more advanced studies by mastering basic English.

"Basic English" here means the language that is used in everyday casual conversation (as illustrated by the advanced reading samples on page 53 of this book and on page 6 of the *Where to Start* booklet). "Basic English" does not include the ability to read Shakespeare, biology textbooks, or other sophisticated material.

ESL:

English as a Second Language

ESL Preview
(Understand and Speak)

Definition

English as a Second Language, or ESL, means the study of English by those who grew up speaking any language other than English. For them, English is a foreign, or second, language (or perhaps a third or fourth language).

ESL Students

The main goal of ESL students is obviously to understand and speak English. They may also have personal goals related to what they hope to accomplish with their English.

Some ESL students are highly educated in their native language. Others have no formal education in any language; they are learning English and basic skills at the same time. Some ESL students can speak reasonably well but can't read or write. Others can actually read better than they can speak.

LITSTART includes guidance for all these situations.

ESL Tutoring

Most ESL tutors don't speak their students' native language. All of the instruction is in English. ESL tutors help their students not only to speak and understand English, but to read and write English and to understand American culture as well.

Literacy Preview
(Read and Write)

Definition

Over the years, definitions of literacy have varied from the ability to write one's name to the completion of a number of years of school.

Most of today's definitions refer to the ability to read and write well enough to function independently in society. This means that a person who was "literate" a century ago might be deemed "functionally illiterate" today because of higher demands of society.

Many modern definitions of literacy also include references to math, speaking English, achieving goals, or using a computer, but in this book, literacy refers simply to basic reading and writing skills.

Literacy Students

Literacy students can be native English speakers or ESL students who have mastered the basics of the spoken language.

The biggest cause of illiteracy among native English speakers is an environment of poverty, an environment that often includes poorly educated parents, poor schools, a lack of enrichment activities, and low expectations. A second cause is personal childhood barriers, which might mean physical or mental impairments, learning disabilities, abuse, or dysfunctional families.

Regardless of the cause, adults who seek literacy help are motivated and can improve their literacy skills.

Literacy Tutoring

Literacy tutors help not only with reading and writing, but also with vocabulary, comprehension, and background knowledge about basic subjects.

Functional literacy: the ability to read and write well enough to function independently in society.

Tutoring Tips

Partnership

Treat your student like any other adult.

Make your student your partner so that you are two peers working together. Make decisions together.

Include your student in the planning process. Ask for your student's opinion and preference in selecting materials, activities, and priorities. Give your student choices.

Highlight talents that your student has—such as cooking, mechanics, art, or music—to help equalize your relationship.

Include your student in the planning process.

Mistakes

Tell your student not to worry about mistakes. Mistakes are helpful; they tell you what to work on. Mistakes are opportunities to learn.

When the student makes an error:

- Say "that's close" or "that's a tricky one" or "try again," rather than "no" or "that's wrong" (see page 11).

- Put the blame on the language. Remind the student that English often violates its own rules.

- Try to identify what information the student misunderstood. Show the student the source of the error.

If you notice a pattern in your student's errors, create a list of samples, show the student the error, and practice correcting it.

If *you* make a mistake, say so; let your student see that it is okay to make mistakes. If you don't know an answer, say so. Research the answer later if you can.

Questions

Before explaining a concept, ask questions to get your student thinking. After explaining a concept, ask questions to make sure your student understands. Encourage your student to ask questions.

Faces

Watch your student's face and body language. If you detect puzzlement, reteach; if you see frustration, change activities; if you see enlightenment, rejoice; if you see pride, build on it.

Student's Notebook

Your student might need guidance in organizing notes and information. If so, suggest that your student use a notebook. Show your student how to use dividers and how to label and date papers.

Seating

Sit beside your student (unless your student is uncomfortable with this) or around the corner of a table; work together.

If you are both right-handed, sit on your student's right so that your hand does not block the student's view when you write or point. However, when your student writes, you might want to move to the left so that your student's hand doesn't block *your* view. If you or your student is left-handed, do the opposite.

New Ideas

If you have a new idea for your lesson, do what good tutors do: try it! If it works, do it again. If it doesn't work, modify it or abandon it.

Throughout your tutoring career, be on the lookout for new ideas, strategies, and materials; and stay in touch with literacy organizations, other tutors, and education professionals. You might also check the Web site of the National Institute for Literacy (www.nifl.gov), which has information on discussion groups, research, conferences, and other resources.

If you detect puzzlement, reteach;

if you see frustration, change activities;

if you see enlightenment, rejoice;

if you see pride, build on it.

Golden Rules for Tutoring Adults

As you tutor, you will face choices both before and during the lesson:

Should I correct that minor error or let it pass?
Should we spend more time on this or should we move on?
Should we work on spelling or reading?

These questions can be answered by applying the three golden rules:

Abandon perfectionism. You don't have the time.

1. Student's Goals

Focus on the goals of the student. Does the activity you are questioning directly relate to a goal or would some other activity be more direct?

2. The 85% Rule

Strive to make your student 80 to 90% successful.

If your student consistently achieves 100%, the work is too easy. Adjust by going faster, changing books, adding harder questions, skipping easy sections, or raising your standards.

If your student is achieving 70%, the work is too difficult. Adjust by slowing down, changing books, adding easy questions, skipping difficult sections, supplying more help, or ignoring minor errors.

3. The 100-Hour Rule

Abandon perfectionism. You don't have the time. Even if you meet your student for two hours a week for a year, you have only 100 hours (50 x 2), the equivalent of two and a half work weeks (40 + 40 + 20). That's not much time.

Are you using your minutes wisely? Language can be a life-and-death issue. Which is more important: understanding apostrophes or understanding a sign that says "high voltage"? Skip the frills. Ignore minor errors. Abandon perfectionism. Focus on survival.

Right and Wrong Things to Say

10 Ways to Say "Good"

You're doing great.	Fantastic! Keep up the good work.
Outstanding!	How did you do that so fast?
Beautiful.	You must have been practicing!
That's right!	Now you've got it.
Nice going.	You just taught me something.

10 Right Ways to Say "Wrong"

That's close!
Almost!
That's a tricky one.
Let's try that again.
Oops!
Oh, I forgot to explain this.
English has a lot of crazy spellings.
This causes trouble for a lot of people.
Would you like me to do a sample for you?
These questions don't make sense. Let's just skip them.

> *Note the teamwork aspect. Note also how the "blame" falls on the language, the book, or even the tutor, rather than the student.*

10 Things Not to Say

No.
That's wrong.
Don't you remember?
We had this before.
This is really easy.
I explained this last week.
Don't you get it?
Everybody knows this.
You're not concentrating.
You have to try harder.

2 The Adult Learner

"It hurts. You have a child and she comes up to you and says, 'Read this,' and 'Read that,' and you can't. It hurts."

—Paula, an adult literacy student

The Adult Learner

This chapter describes adult learners, their learning styles, and the special problems that some of them have:

A Diverse Population

Understanding the adult learner will increase your effectiveness.

Adult students have diverse backgrounds:

- a nurse from Asia working now as a custodian
- a truck driver with a high school diploma
- an unemployed high school drop-out from an impoverished home
- a seamstress from Mexico with only five years of education
- an owner of a small business
- a dishwasher with a hearing impairment

Adult students have diverse goals:

- to get a driver's license
- to help a child with homework
- to speak English better
- to be able to write checks
- to prepare to take the GED Test
- to get a better job
- to be able to read the sports section of the paper
- to read the Bible
- to become a U. S. citizen
- to spell better
- to fill out daily report sheets at work
- to fulfill a lifelong dream to learn to read

Adult students have diverse abilities:

- reads easy material but stumbles on longer words
- speaks only a few words of English
- speaks well, but has trouble with even simple reading
- recognizes many words but has poor comprehension
- reads English fairly well, but doesn't speak well
- reads well in a native language but not English
- reads well but has trouble with spelling

"Learning to read is like coming out of the dark."

Students Speak Out...

The following quotes, from interviews and writings of real students, illustrate opinions and feelings that your student may share.

... on life without basic skills

"You learn different techniques to get around the [reading] problem. If you get stuck in a situation where you don't know what you are doing, you make up an excuse to leave."

"I want learn English for help my daughter."

"I know I could have made foreman, but I shied way from applying because I knew sooner or later, I'd have to read."

"I was in this foxhole with a kid from New York. I got my mail and handed it to him to read. He said, 'I can't read,' and I said, 'I can't read either.'"

"In my country, school is not for girls. Here, ... I can learn"

"The school ... was not a real school. ... It had no desks in it. We had to put our books on our legs. ... It was about fifty children and one teacher. And he would drink wine and sleep most of the day."

... on education

"My tutor thinks I could go to college some day."

"Learning to read is like coming out of the dark."

"Education is the most wonderful thing that ever happened to me, other than my marriage and my children."

"Before I started this program, I could not talk to you. Now I can talk to anyone."

"I'm doing things I never thought I could do."

"I thank God for this fantastic opportunity. I thought just to be able to read was it, but I found out that reading makes me very happy. To be able to read is everything. ... I care about tomorrow because tomorrow is another word and another book!"

Characteristics of Adult Learners

Despite their differences, most adults share certain characteristics that make teaching them different from teaching children:

Language English-speaking adults have a broad vocabulary and an awareness of the patterns of English. Fewer words have to be explained than for children. ESL students have their native language to use for reference.

Knowledge Adults possess a wealth of knowledge about life, work, people, music, sports, business, politics, and a thousand other things. This "prior knowledge" serves as a rich basis for conversation, for comprehension of reading material, and for inspiration for writing.

Priorities Adult students may have urgent survival needs or other important goals. Personal goals should have priority over general improvement.

Time Most adults have responsibilities that restrict their time. This means study time should be productive and focus on critical skills.

Control Since adults are used to making decisions and are aware of their needs, they should be involved in the selection of materials and activities. Their opinions, preferences, and priorities should be respected.

Content Adults generally wish to study materials designed for adults. Finding appropriate content can be difficult, especially for beginning readers.

Self-image Adults who do not speak or read well often suffer more daily frustration than other adults. Although everyone appreciates support, adult students need it in a special way.

Motivation Adults come to tutoring sessions voluntarily, which means they are already motivated. Motivation will be maintained if the student sees success and progress toward personal goals.

Learning Styles: An Overview

Just as people have different tastes in music and art, people also have different preferences in the way they learn. For example, some people prefer to study in a quiet room; others learn better through a lively discussion. The more closely you can tailor your tutoring to your student's preferred style, the faster your student will learn.

Learning styles have many dimensions, as the chart below shows. The pages that follow elaborate on these dimensions.

1. **Perceptual** .... how the brain receives information
2. **Processing** .... how the brain processes information
3. **Environmental** .... how the surroundings affect the body
4. **Physical** .... how the body feels
5. **Emotional** .... how the mind feels

Your student's learning style may be different from yours.

What to Do About Learning Styles

Don't make any special effort to classify your student's learning style right away. Just observe, listen, and watch for patterns.

- Be careful not to impose your style on your student. Instead of saying, "I'll close the window," say, "Would you rather have the window opened or closed?"

- Try to accommodate any request your student makes—from changing pens to talking more slowly.

- Experiment with tutoring strategies that appeal to different learning styles.

- Abandon strategies that frustrate your student.

- Talk to your student, at some point, about learning styles and ask your student to think about what works best.

1. Perceptual Dimensions

Visual, Auditory, Kinesthetic, Tactile (VAKT)

When people say, "If I see it, I'll remember it," or "I have to write it down or I'll forget it," they are indicating their perceptual learning style. **We all use all four styles** (visual, auditory, kinesthetic, and tactile), but some people have a favorite.

Visual Learners Often:

- Recall images or words after seeing them a few times.
- Notice visual details, design, and spelling errors.
- Discriminate easily between words that look alike (cat/act).

Implications for tutoring:

Use written instructions and examples, not just oral ones. Use pictures and diagrams. Try Strategies 16, 18, 23, 24, 25, 33, 39, and 40.

Auditory Learners Often:

- Recall information after hearing it a few times.
- Discriminate between words that sound alike (bat/pat).

Implications for tutoring:

Use tapes, discussions, and oral explanations. Encourage the student to read aloud, think aloud, and spell aloud. Use phonics. Try Strategies 15, 16, 19, 20, 26-30, 32, 36-38, and 43.

Kinesthetic and Tactile Learners Often:

- Recall words after writing or typing them a few times.
- Are good with their hands or good at sports.

Implications for tutoring:

Use writing or typing to answer questions and review words. Act out stories or move objects to aid in comprehension. "Write" on the table with a finger. Tap out syllables. Try Strategies 26, 33-35, 39, 41, and 50.

2. Processing Dimensions

The two hemispheres of the brain are responsible for different tasks. Although some people mix left and right-brained thinking skills evenly (below), other people seem to have a "favorite" side.

Detail ("Left Brain")..........................Holistic ("Right Brain")

←——————————————————————————————————————→

Structure, organization.. *Free form*
Details .... **General** ideas
Sequence ....Randomness
Schedules, rules .... Spontaneity, creativity
Analysis: breaking down .... *Synthesis: building up*
Logic and reason................................... *Feelings* and intuition
Punctual .... ~~Time~~ is not important
Conventional.. *U n c o n v e n t i o n a l*
Neat, straight............................... Sc att er ed, clutteredddd
Math, grammar, spelling .... *Art*, music, **drama**
Files .... Piles

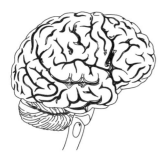

Implications for tutoring:

Detail (Left-Brained) Learners

Detail students usually like rules, phonics, spelling, dictation sentences, workbooks, and lists. They would rather study difficult words before reading. Comprehension may be a problem if the student focuses too much on individual words. Try Strategies 14, 23, and 24. Left-hemisphere learners like to measure their progress. Writing may be difficult because being creative involves risk. Try Strategies 53-57 at first for comfort. Introduce the other writing strategies gently to encourage fluency.

Holistic (Right-Brained) Learners

Right-hemisphere students respond to the whole text (Strategies 15, 18, 20, and 25). They prefer to read first and study words afterward. Phonics is too tedious for many holistic learners; they may learn better by sight. Spelling will not be easy. Experiment with a variety of strategies. For writing, right-brained learners respond well to Strategies 50, 51, 52, 58, and 59.

3. Environmental Dimensions

Light Some readers like bright lights; others prefer dim (see page 23).

Sound Some people like background music; others need quiet. Use a fan to cover unavoidable background noise.

Temperature Make your student comfortable.

Openness Having doors and windows open or closed may affect the student's ability to concentrate.

Furnishings Formal atmospheres please some but intimidate others.

4. Physical Dimensions

Position While some people like to sit at a desk when they read, others like to relax in an easy chair.

Strength Students whose eyes or hands tire quickly while reading or writing need to build muscle strength gradually. Rest every few minutes if needed.

Intake Arrange for breaks to meet your student's needs for snacks, beverages, or nicotine. Perhaps a beverage can be kept at the table.

Time If possible, meet in the morning for a "morning person" and in the evening for a "night person."

Mobility Students who are restless may need frequent breaks.

5. Emotional Dimensions

Motivation Most students are self-motivated, but some may need an extra incentive now and then. See page 196.

Persistence Some students prefer a consistent, predictable lesson; others thrive on the excitement of variety.

Some students have special problems.

Hearing Problems

Symptoms:

- Talking loudly
- Asking you to repeat
- Frequently not "remembering" what you said
- Misunderstanding you
- Turning one ear toward you when you talk
- Not hearing you at all if you are not facing each other

Implications for tutoring:

- Encourage the student to have a hearing check.
- Enunciate clearly.
- Speak loudly, but don't yell.
- Sit on the student's "good side."
- Make sure the student is looking at you when you speak.
- Eliminate as much background noise as possible.
- Ask the student to repeat things back to you.

Vision Problems

Symptoms:

- Squinting
- Holding the book very close or far away
- Bending low over the table
- Headache
- Eye fatigue
- Inability to distinguish small print

Implications for tutoring:

- Encourage the student to have a vision check.
- Ask the student to tell you when the print is too small.
- Work in a well-lit area.
- Check the library for large-print books.
- Enlarge small type on a copy machine.
- Try magnifying sheets or "reading" (magnifying) glasses.

Sensitivity to Light

Symptoms:

- Tendency to shield the eyes with hands, a hat, or sunglasses
- Comments about words running together or moving
- Watery, burning, or itchy eyes during reading
- Complaints about glare

Implications for tutoring:

If you think your student may be sensitive to light, suggest to your student that you jointly try the techniques below and look for any relief of symptoms.

- Dim the lights or sit far from the light.
- Use sunglasses or a hat with a large brim.
- Compare the effects of different lighting. Fluorescent is usually the worst; incandescent is better; indirect sunlight is best.
- Make copies of a page on different colors of paper. Compare the effect.
- Try reading through different colors of filters. (Office supply stores sell plastic report covers that work well.) Let the student select the color that works best.

> *If your student has special problems, you can, in general, use the same techniques as you use with other students.*

Learning Disabilities (LD)

"Learning disability" is a broad term covering a number of learning problems associated with the way the brain processes information. People can have problems with reading (dyslexia), penmanship, math, or other skills.

People with learning disabilities (LD) often have average or above average intelligence and may have outstanding talents in other areas. This makes their learning difficulties in one particular area seem puzzling. (In contrast, people with mental impairments have difficulty in all areas of learning.)

(It may be useful to know that persons who are officially diagnosed as learning disabled have certain rights, especially regarding employment, under the Americans with Disabilities Act. Employers must provide certain accommodations such as a tape recorder or extra time.)

People with Learning Disabilities (LD) just Learn Differently (LD).

Dyslexia

Dyslexia is the learning disability associated with reading. Experts disagree on the definition, causes, extent, types, and treatment of dyslexia, but research is gradually clarifying the issue.

The main symptom of dyslexia is simply that the person persistently struggles with reading despite normal intelligence, adequate instruction, and a lack of any other logical explanation. Other symptoms vary. Some people have problems with letter reversals, penmanship, spelling, comprehension, or coordination. But, of course, many people experience these "other symptoms" without being dyslexic.

There is, as yet, no cure for dyslexia, but determined students can learn to read. Various suggested techniques usually involve lots of tutoring, often using many of the strategies that are in this book. The key is to think about learning styles, try different strategies, monitor progress, and involve your student in the evaluation of what works and what doesn't.

Implications for tutoring:

If you think your student might be dyslexic or otherwise learning disabled, you may feel that you do not have the expertise to help. But, in practical terms, you may be the best resource available. Try some of the following techniques.

- Check up on the latest research if you wish, but maintain a healthy skepticism and check several sources. Remember, the experts disagree.

- Check your student's sensitivity to light (page 23).

- Experiment with different strategies and learning styles. Whatever your student enjoys is probably also helpful.

  - Some people respond to traditional techniques (Strategies 14, 21, and 22) done more slowly, in shorter segments, and with more repetition.

  - Others enjoy kinesthetic and tactile techniques (Strategies 26, 33-35, 39, 41, and 50).

  - Some like intensive phonics (Strategies 26-29).

  - Others respond to word families or sight words.

  - Still others learn best with holistic approaches (Strategies 15, 18, 20, and 25).

- Using all the senses often helps: seeing, hearing/saying, and writing the words.

- Use books with large, clear type, or enlarge the text on a copier.

- Take frequent mini-breaks. Learning disabilities intensify with stress or fatigue.

- Encourage your student to point to the words or to hold a card under the line of text while reading if that helps.

- Just be there. Many students make their best progress when someone is at their side to supply constant feedback about whether the words are right or wrong.

- Be patient. Working with a learning disability takes time.

- Involve your student in deciding which strategies work best.

Involve your student in deciding which strategies work best.

3 Your First Session

" Some people wish they could have a million dollars. I wish I could read."

--- *Rick, an adult literacy student*

Your First Session

This chapter will provide you with an outline for the first lesson and with a placement guide to determine your student's initial skill level:

Getting Ready

If you are nervous about your first meeting, just remember that your student is probably even more so. Focus on making your student feel comfortable, appreciated, and optimistic.

Objectives of the First Session
1. To establish trust
2. To learn about your student
3. To give the student an experience of success

Contacting Your Student

If you are responsible for making the initial contact with your student, you will probably call to arrange your first meeting. (If your student knows no English, ask your literacy coordinator for a translator to help with the first call.) When your student answers:

1. Introduce yourself. Ask if this is a good time to talk.

2. Tell the student you are looking forward to working together. Explain that at the first meeting you will make plans and talk.

3. Select a day and a time that is convenient for both of you.

4. Select a quiet location such as a library, church, school, community center, or business. Small private rooms are best. Avoid meeting in a home because of distractions and liability issues. If you need help finding a site, contact your coordinator.

5. Give your student your telephone number, slowly. Ask the student to call if there will be a problem making a session.

If your student is not home, call back later. Don't discuss tutoring business with family members unless you have the student's consent.

The primary purpose of the first lesson is to establish trust.

Materials for Your First Lesson
- Lined paper, pencils, pens, eraser
- LITSTART and the *Where to Start* booklet
- Forms or materials supplied by your literacy organization
- World map and simple objects (for ESL)

First Session for ESL Students

1. Introduction

Smile and introduce yourself. Encourage your student to respond. Make sure you are pronouncing the student's name correctly. Sit down and invite your student to sit near you. (Let your student control the relative position of the chairs.) Try a little small talk about the weather, the room, or learning English. See how the student responds.

2. Map

Using simple sentences, show the student your state and city on a world map. Show where your family is from. Then ask where your student is from. Together, find your student's country. Ask simple questions about the country to try to start a discussion.

If the student has trouble, just point and say simple sentences. "This is the United States." Encourage the student to repeat your words.

—Check Point—

If your student converses with you easily and speaks in complete sentences (not necessarily perfect), switch to Step 1 on the next page. Otherwise, continue with Step 3 below.

3. Ability Level

Use the *Where to Start* exercise on page 36 to determine a starting level for your student. (If your student knows no English, your student is at the ESL 1 level. Move on to Step 4.)

4. Objects

Using Strategy 1 on page 79, discuss a few objects that you brought or that are in the room.

5. Story

Review the sentences generated in Step 4. Write them in a paragraph form. Read it to the student. Give the paragraph to the student.

6. Conclusion

Express how pleased you are with the student's efforts. Your words may not be understood, but your smile will be!

First Session for Literacy Students

1. Introduction

Smile and introduce yourself. Make sure you are pronouncing the student's name correctly.

Make the student comfortable. Adjust the door, window, light, temperature, and seating to the student's liking.

Set your student at ease by saying something like:

> I am here to help you learn **whatever you want to learn.** We can work on whatever you want to work on.

> If you want to **bring anything** from home or from work to read or talk about, just bring it. If you get any mail that you want help with, just bring it, and that will be our lesson.

> I will need your help. We'll work together as a **team**, okay? If I go too slow or too fast, let me know; or if something I say doesn't make sense, just say so; or if you don't like the materials we are using, just tell me, and we'll find something else.

> Don't worry about **mistakes.** You can make all the mistakes you want. Mistakes help us learn. I'll probably make some mistakes too.

> Whenever you have any **questions**, just ask. Questions are good. How does that sound? Do you have any questions now?

> It will take us a little time to get to know each other and to **experiment** with different books and activities, but if you'll help me out, we'll make good progress, I'm sure.

> **Today** we'll just get to know each other and try a few things, okay?

Literacy Students

1. Introduction

2. Chat

3. Goals

4. Ability Level

5. Experience Story

6. Conclusion

"How far did you get in school?"

2. Chat

Get to know each other. Tell a little about yourself, but focus on the student. Show interest, but do not probe. Follow any topic the student introduces. Questions you might ask are:

School: How far did you get in school?
Did you like school? Why or why not?
What were your favorite subjects?

Family: Do you have a family? Tell me about them.
How long have you lived here?

Interests: What do you do in your spare time?
What kinds of TV shows do you like to watch?

Job: What type of work do you do?
Do you like your job? Why or why not?

Ability: What things are you good at?

3. Goals

Explain that you would like to start a list of things the student wants to learn (see samples on pages 33, 34, 48, 56, and 58). Ask the student to help you think of items for the list as you continue your conversation. (This Master Topics List will be crucial to future lesson planning.)

"What kinds of things would you like to be able to read?"

General: What do you especially want to learn?
What will you do with the new skills you learn?

Speaking: (If ESL) Do you speak English at home? at work?
at the store? Where else?
What times do you need English the most?

Reading: What things would you like to be able to read?
Do you need to read mail? signs? things at work?

Writing: What kinds of things would you like to write?
Do you need to write at work? or fill out forms?
Do you want to work on spelling?

Priorities: What things on this list should we work on first?
(Read items to or with the student.
Check [✔] items the student selects.)

Sample Master Topics List Based on Student's Goals

Tony is a father of three and a custodian. He wants to learn English so he can improve his life and help his family.

Conversation ideas with priority topics checked (✔):

- job:
    - ✔ - talk better with supervisor
        - problems with equipment
        - work hours
    - talk better with co-workers

- children's school:
    - talk better with teacher
    - talk with other parents at school events

- finances:
    - how to save money at bank
    - how to talk to clerk at bank

- other:
    - ✔ - talk better to doctor
    - ✔ - get help at drug store
    - talk to bus driver
    - ask directions

Reading ideas:

- children's school:
    - help children with homework (reading, spelling)
    - understand notes from school

- other:
    - understand bills
    - read other mail

> *Your student's goals will serve as the basis for your lesson plans.*

Sample Master Topics Lists Based on Students' Goals

Jerry's main goal is to read to his grandson.

Reading ideas with priority items checked (✔):
- ✔ children's books
- stories about grandparents with grandchildren
- general interest

Writing ideas with priority items checked (✔):
- ✔ list of children's books practiced
- stories of own life to read to grandson
- journal of experiences with grandson
- notes to grandson

Michelle's goal is to pass the GED Test.

The GED Test is beyond your mission as a tutor. However, you can help your student improve reading and writing skills to prepare for enrolling in a GED class. (The GED Test consists of five parts: Literature, Writing, Social Studies, Science, and Math.)

Reading ideas with priority items checked (✔):
- ✔ fiction
- newspaper and magazine articles
- basic science, such as
    - animal functions and behaviors
    - health issues
    - environmental issues
- ✔ basic social studies, such as
    - stories from U.S. history
    - current events

Writing ideas:
- summaries of articles read
- opinions about people and events
- a journal

4. Ability Level

If you have no information on the student's ability, use the *Where to Start* exercise on page 36 to establish a rough ability level.

If you already know your student's level from another source, you can use *Where to Start* just to get a better idea of the student's abilities and needs.

5. Experience Story

The Experience Story (Strategy 18) is a possible exercise for the first meeting unless your student speaks very little English or is an advanced reader. It will not only give the student a successful experience, but it will tell you more about your student.

6. Conclusion

- Summarize what you have learned about the student's interests and needs. Thank the student for helping you.

- Talk about ideas for the next lesson based on the goals you identified together (Step 3). You might plan to look for materials related to the student's interests; the student might bring materials from home or work; or you might go together to the library, literacy office, or book store.

- Remind the student that it may take a few weeks to find the right materials and the best way to work together.

- Ask the student for questions or suggestions.

- Confirm the time, date, and place of your next meeting.

- Congratulate the student on a job well done.

1. Introduction

2. Chat

3. Goals

4. Ability Level

5. Experience Story

6. Conclusion

The *Where to Start* Placement Guide

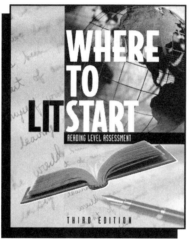

Included with your LITSTART book is a small booklet called *Where to Start*. The purpose of *Where to Start* is to place your student in one of five levels. Knowing this level will help you plan your lessons. *(Where to Start* is designed to show only a starting level, not progress.)

Student Ability Levels

LITSTART's strategies are based on a five-level system in which two ESL levels precede three literacy levels. As the chart indicates, ESL 2 students may receive a little literacy instruction and advanced ESL speakers can receive the same instruction as literacy students.

Level	ESL	Literacy
1	Beginning speaker (ESL 1)	
2	Intermediate speaker (ESL 2)	(Beginning reader)
3	Advanced speaker ⟶	Beginning reader
4	Advanced speaker ⟶	Intermediate reader
5		Advanced reader

The five levels are described in more detail later in this chapter and in Chapter 4.

Where to Start has four exercises:

> Speaking Exercise (for ESL)
> Letters and Sounds Exercise
> Reading Exercise
> Spelling Exercise

The instructions are on the following pages.

Speaking Exercise

This exercise will give you an idea of the speaking abilities of your ESL student. It will identify your student as ESL 1, ESL 2, or beyond. (If your student is a native speaker of English, start with the Reading Exercise on page 41.)

ESL Level 1

ESL 1 students range from those who know no English at all to those who can convey simple ideas by stringing three or four words together, but rarely in correct sentences: "Me go store." "Where coffee?"

ESL Level 2

ESL 2 students range from those who can string simple thoughts together ("Me go store." "Where coffee?") to those who speak in sentences that are almost correct ("I go to store yesterday." "Where is coffee, please?"). The sentences may be brief, the grammar imperfect, and the accent strong, but the student is generally understandable.

Students who are beyond ESL 2 are ready to progress into literacy instruction (reading and writing). Literacy instruction will help them improve their vocabulary and grammar. If you have an advanced ESL student, you can include some speaking instruction in your lessons if you wish.

Preparations for the Speaking Exercise

Before beginning, say something like "I have some pictures for you. Let's talk about these pictures."

During the exercise (described on next page), there are four things you should do:

- Nod or say "good" or "right" frequently.
- Listen carefully. You will start to get a feel for the student's strengths and weaknesses.
- If the student makes a minor error, don't point it out. Just listen.
- If the student doesn't know an answer, supply it. (This is not a test.) **At that point, you will have identified the ability level and begun instruction at the same time.**

Students who are beyond ESL Level 2 are ready to progress into literacy instruction.

page 1

Instructions for Page 1 of *Where to Start*

Show your student page 1 in the *Where to Start* booklet. Ask the questions below, taking care not to give hints at first. Wait. Then if the student needs help, supply it and continue giving help as needed.

Your Question	Minimum Response
Row 1: Understanding simple nouns 1. Where is the car? (Don't even point to the first row.) 2. Where is the dog?	The student should point to the object. (Any verbal response is extra data for you.)
Row 2: Saying simple nouns 3. What is this? (Use your pen to point to the key.) 4. What are these? (Point to the shoes.) 5. What is this? (Point to the house.)	The student should give the word or a description ("lock door"). Mimicking the motion doesn't count.
Row 3: Saying simple verbs and phrases 6. What is she doing? (Point to the woman.) 7. What is he doing? (Point to the man.) 8. What is this? (Point to the hands.)	The student should say at least two appropriate words such as "talk phone" or "man call."

Page 1 Results

If your student answered all the questions without help, go on to page 2 of *Where to Start*.

If your student needed help, your student is at ESL Level 1. Stop the *Where to Start* exercise here and return to your lesson plan (page 30).

If in doubt, go ahead and try page 2. Remember, this is not a test; it is simply a tool to give you an idea of the student's needs.

Instructions for Page 2

Show your student page 2 in the *Where to Start* booklet.

1. Ask the student what the first person is doing. (You may wish to write down the student's responses for later analysis.)
2. Continue with the remaining pictures.

page 2

Page 2 Results

There are not necessarily any right or wrong answers. By hearing your student's responses, you should start to get an idea of your student's limitations and needs. The more complete and accurate your student's responses, the more you can plan to focus on literacy skills rather than on speaking skills in your future lessons (as the three scenarios below illustrate).

If your student omitted many words and endings ("He drink water" or "Boy have milk"), struggled with words, had many errors, or needed help, your student is at ESL Level 2. Try the Letters and Sounds Exercise on the next page. Your future lessons should probably focus more on speaking than on literacy unless the student's goals suggest otherwise.

If your student used sentences that were almost correct and often five or more words in length ("This is boy with glass water" or "He have a glass in the hand"), your student has enough speaking ability to profit from some literacy instruction. Proceed to the Letters and Sounds Exercise. Plan to devote about half of your future lesson time to speaking (ESL 2) and half to literacy (at your student's reading level). Adjust this timing according to your student's goals.

If most of your student's responses were complete and grammatically correct ("This is a boy drinking a glass of milk"), your student is beyond ESL 2. Plan to focus on literacy, although you may still include some speaking instruction in your lessons to meet specific needs. Your student's speaking skills will improve through reading and writing instruction. Proceed to the Letters and Sounds Exercise.

Letters and Sounds Exercise

Use this exercise for ESL 2 and beginning literacy students only. You may wish to write down the letters and sounds the student knows.

1. Ask the student to tell you the names of the letters. Supply help if needed.

2. If the student succeeds, ask for the sounds of the consonants. (You may have to give an example. The concept is new to some students.)

3. If the student succeeds, ask for the long and short sounds of the vowels. (Expect nothing. Very few students know these.)

p	b	s	z
t	d	f	v
m	n	g	k
j	c	w	h
r	l	y	x
qu	sh	ch	th

a e i o u

page 3

Letters and Sounds Exercise Results

The student's errors will show you what skills need work. You can begin instruction during or immediately after the exercise if you wish.

Even if the student did poorly on this exercise, proceed to the Reading Exercise (if you have not already tried it). Many students can read reasonably well without being able to say the sounds in isolation.

Reading Exercise

This exercise will help determine your student's general reading level.

Before beginning, set the student at ease by saying things like:

- "We need to figure out where to start. **Would you help me** by doing a little sample reading?" (Show the student page 4 in the *Where to Start* booklet.)

- "This is not a test. I'll help you if you get stuck."

During the reading:

- Nod or say "good" or "right" frequently.

- Listen carefully. You will start to get a sense of the student's strengths and weaknesses.

- If the student makes a minor error, don't point it out. But note that **you have determined the starting level.**

- If the student gets stuck, wait a minute, then say the word. (This is not the time for a phonics lesson.) Note that **you have determined the starting level and you have begun instruction simultaneously.** Continue the story, giving assistance as needed.

After each passage:

- **Important**: Ask what the story was about.

- If the student had any difficulty reading or explaining the story, stop. Otherwise, proceed to the next story.

Reading Exercise Results

Discuss your observations with the student ("It seems like the first story was easy for you, and it would be good if we could practice more stories that are like this second story. What do you think?").

The page that first caused difficulty indicates the student's starting level:

- Difficulty reading or explaining page 4 .... Beginning level
- Difficulty reading or explaining page 5 .... Intermediate level
- Difficulty reading or explaining page 6 .... Advanced level
- No difficulty with page 6 .... Beyond advanced

If in doubt, use the lower level. It's better to start too low than too high.

If your student is at the beginning level, check the student's letters and sounds on the preceding page, if you have not already done so.

Whatever your student's level, proceed to the Spelling Exercise.

beginning level

Tom's Car

page 4

intermediate level

Moving Up

page 5

advanced level

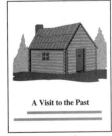

A Visit to the Past

page 6

Spelling Exercise

To determine your student's spelling level, ask your student to write the words that you say. Emphasize that this is not a test; it's just practice.

- Pronounce each word clearly and use it in a sentence:
  1. cat   My cat likes to sleep.   cat

- Repeat the word as many times as the student needs it.

- If the student gets stuck or misspells a word, help the student correct the word immediately. **You will then have identified the level and will have begun instruction.** Continue with the next word in that column.

- If your student made any errors, stop at the end of that column. If your student made no errors, continue with the next column. Either way, congratulate your student on the correct words.

"This is not a test; it's just practice."

Beginning	Intermediate	Advanced
1. cat	6. think	16. caught
2. ten	7. lunch	17. completed
3. pack	8. flight	18. picture
4. shop	9. glasses	19. computer
5. ring	10. stopped	20. December
	11. dried	21. supervisor
	12. said	22. promise
	13. does	23. people
	14. spoil	24. Wednesday
	15. woman	25. although

Spelling Exercise Results

The column in which your student first missed any words or needed help marks the level at which you can begin spelling instruction.

If your student spelled all the words correctly, read the most advanced story easily, and does not need assistance on a particularly special goal, your student is beyond the basic skill level for which this program was designed. The student should move on to a more advanced program. Check with your literacy organization.

4 Planning Your Tutoring Sessions

"My brain has come back to life."

—Ora Lee, an adult literacy student

Planning Your Tutoring Sessions

This chapter will provide you with general guidelines and steps for planning your sessions as well as specific checklists and ideas for each of the five skill levels:

Ready to Plan

At your first meeting you gathered information about your student's background, interests, and goals. You also determined your student's general ability level.

Your focus now is to find the best combination of materials and activities within your student's ability level to meet your student's goals. This chapter will guide you through a three-step process to develop a lesson that will accomplish this. Your lesson will have up to three parts for literacy students and up to four parts for ESL students:

Parts of a Lesson

1. **Speaking (for ESL)**
2. **Reading**
3. **Word Study**
4. **Writing**

These four parts are discussed in detail in Chapters 5, 6, 7, and 8, respectively.

Your next few tutoring sessions will involve much preparation and experimentation. Each session will provide you with data that you can use to make the following lesson even better. Revise your routine as you identify materials and activities that work well for you and your student. Not all activities work with all students, but your LITSTART book is full of alternative ideas.

As you develop a routine, the preparation will take less time.

Each lesson will provide you with data that you can use to make the following lesson even better.

Planning Parameters

Lesson length   An hour is the limit of concentration for some students; others can handle two hours or more if they get a break and a change of activities. Experiment.

Frequency   The more often you meet, the better. One session per week is good, but if you can meet twice a week, your student's progress will be more than doubled.

Timing   For ESL, spend most of the time on speaking. For most literacy students, spend about 50% of the time on reading, 25% on word study, and 25% on writing. You can modify this allocation to adjust for urgent needs or special interests.

Sequence   The sequence of (1) speaking, (2) reading, (3) word study, and (4) writing has no special significance. Adjust it according to your preference.

Caution #1   Beware of over-socializing. Use a few minutes to nurture friendship and keep up with the student's needs and interests or to take a break, but be careful not to chatter your valuable tutoring time away. Exceptions: (1) ESL, where speaking is the goal, and (2) discussing factual information that will increase your student's knowledge base.

Caution #2   Remember that your job is to tutor, not to counsel. If your student has personal problems, talk to your literacy organization about professional assistance.

Caution #3   Beware of consistently "running out of time" before the last part of the lesson. This often happens when either the tutor or the student is secretly reluctant to try that activity. Fear not! Adjust your timing and forge ahead!

Planning Tips

Include your student in the planning process.

Let your student select the topics. Ask your student to bring materials from home. Take your student to the library or literacy office to select books. Offer your student two or three books. Which one does your student like best? Try a strategy. What does your student think of it? Did it help? If not, try a different technique next time. Give your student choices. Ask for your student's opinion.

Prepare significantly more material than you expect to cover.

This not only safeguards you from running out of material, but it also improves your tutoring. You will do a far better job if you think, "How are we going to cover all this material?" than if you think, "How am I going to stretch this out to fill the time?"

With a new student or new material, err on the side of planning work that is too easy rather than too difficult.

This gives your student, who may be apprehensive, a feeling of success rather than failure as you fine-tune your techniques.

Find a routine that works for you and your student.

This not only saves you time but it also gives your student a degree of comfort with the lesson. To find a routine, experiment with different strategies and materials until you find a few that work well. Then use the same strategies and materials as your core lesson at every session, gradually increasing the difficulty of the words and subject matter.

Finding a routine may take from five to ten lessons. Of course, even the best routine will have to be adjusted as a student's skills improve or as you complete sets of material.

Include your student in the planning process.

1. Select Topics

2. Select Materials

3. Select Strategies

Three Steps for Planning a Session

Step 1: Select Topics

Your first step in planning your tutoring sessions is to review the Master Topics List that you created at your first lesson (page 32). The priority items that you checked should be the focus of your next several lessons (see sample below and on pages 33, 34, 56, and 58). Periodically review and revise the Master Topics List and priorities with your student.

Pedro is single. He works in a factory but would like a better job.

Reading ideas with priority topics checked (✓):
- ✓ **stories about different jobs**
- articles on how to find a job
- ✓ **want ads**
- articles on leadership, communication
- brochures from job training schools
- general interest

Writing ideas with priority topics checked (✓):
- ✓ **sample application forms**
- questions to ask at an interview
- ✓ **lists of appealing jobs**
- resume
- letters to prospective employers
- journal of work activities

The checked priority items should be the focus of your next several lessons.

Step 2: Select Materials

Keeping in mind your priority topics from Step 1, search for materials from every possible source. Give some consideration to reading level (see pages 52-53), but don't let the reading level be the overriding concern; if the material is too easy or too difficult, you will compensate by using appropriate tutoring strategies, described later.

Sources of Materials

Your student—Encourage your student to bring mail or other materials from home or work.

Your home—See the next two pages for ideas.

Literacy organization—Ask your literacy coordinator about borrowing or buying books and other materials.

Library—If your library does not have an adult basic reading/ESL collection, ask them to start one. Take a field trip to the library and encourage your student to get a library card.

Youth department—The youth departments of libraries and book stores are rich with easy-to-read **non**fiction, such as biographies, science, and history. Some children's picture books may also be suitable for early ESL. Make sure the book does not use juvenile language or pictures; avoid children's fiction (unless your student's goal is to read to children); and be aware that your student may not feel comfortable browsing among children's books. If in doubt, go alone.

Adult education—Ask adult education programs, ESL centers, or community colleges about borrowing or buying books.

Book stores—Try book stores, garage sales, and used book sales.

Computers—Check the Internet and educational software.

Experience Story—Use Strategy 18 to generate reading material based on the student's life.

Publishers—You can order books from adult education publishers.

Yourself—Use Strategy 17 to rewrite material for your student.

> *Don't let the reading level be the overriding concern.*

Everyday Materials from Home and Work

The materials below can be used as reading material, as conversation starters for ESL, or as inspiration for writing lessons.

Advertisements
Bills
Books
Brochures
Bumper stickers
Bus or subway schedules
Calendars
Catalogs
Containers
    Cans
    Cereal boxes
    Other foods
    Detergent
Cookbooks
Coupons
Dictionary
Forms
    Credit application
    Job application
    Income tax
    Insurance
    Registration
Greeting cards
Identification cards
Instruction booklets
    Appliances
    Games
    Vehicles
Internet
Labels
    Cleaning products
    Clothing
    Medicine bottles
    Tapes, CDs, records
    Toiletries
Magazines
Mail
Maps
Menus

Newsletters
Newspapers
    Advice columns
    Comics
    Letters to editor
    Movie ads and reviews
    News (local, state, national, world)
    Recipes
    Sports
    Store ads
    Travel section
    Want ads
    Weather
Notes from children's school
Program books (plays, concerts, sports)
Recipes
Shopping lists
Signs
    Appendix L
    Appendix M
    Billboards
    Parking and street signs
    Store signs
Song lyrics
Telephone book
Textbooks
TV listings
Vending machine instructions
Work-related materials
    Forms
    Handouts
    Machine manuals
    Memos
    Pay stubs
    Policy books
    Signs
    Union information
Wrappers
Yellow Pages

Everyday ESL Materials

The main "materials" for ESL students are spoken words. Think about the vocabulary that pertains to the student's particular goal. List relevant nouns (car, road), verbs (drive, stop, turn), and other words and phrases (fast, slow, to town, be careful).

In addition to the words and the items on the previous page, other everyday items from home and work can be used to stimulate conversation, to explain American culture, or to illustrate vocabulary.

Calendar
Cartoons
Clock or watch
Color samples
  Children's toys
  Paint chips
  Paper
Items to count
  Checkers
  Game pieces
  Pennies
  Puzzle pieces
Kitchen utensils
Money
  Bills
  Checks
  Coins
Office supplies
  Paper clips, staples
  Pens, pencils, markers
  Stamps, envelopes
Picture books
  Art books
  Children's picture dictionaries
  ESL picture dictionaries
  Travel books showing people

Pictures from:
  Advertisements
  Calendars
  Catalogs
  Computer clip art
  Greeting cards
  Magazines
  Newspapers
  Postcards
  Wrapping paper
Photographs
  Modes of transportation
  People in action
  Rooms of furniture
  Student's family
Shapes
  Cut from paper
  From children's toys
Tools from work
Toy miniatures
  Animals
  Furniture
  People
  Vehicles

LITSTART uses only the broad reading levels of beginning, intermediate, and advanced.

Grade Levels of Reading Materials

Although it would seem that a tutor should select books that match the student's reading grade level, the issue is not that simple.

A book that is rated as second grade level according to one evaluation formula may be on the fifth grade level according to another. Student reading scores can also vary from test to test. Therefore, a book and a student that appear to be on the same level according to one set of tests may differ by five grades according to another set. This is one of the reasons that grade levels should not be given much consideration.

Because of these and other factors, LITSTART uses only the broad reading levels of beginning, intermediate, and advanced. Examples and descriptions of the three literacy levels are on the next page.

How to Match a Book to Your Student's Level

Instead of relying on grade levels, use these techniques:

- Focus primarily on the whether the content relates to your student's goals and interests. (You can later adjust your tutoring strategies according to the relative difficulty for the student.)

- Use the descriptions on the next page to match a book (or other reading material) with the student's general level as determined in the first lesson.

- Take two or three possible reading materials to your tutoring session and encourage your student to bring materials from home. Describe each book and let your student select one to try first.

- Try the selected book using Strategies, 14, 21, and 22, the basic trio of reading strategies. If the book is too difficult, abandon it or switch to strategies designed for difficult material (page 105).

- Use your own good judgment. After just a few lessons with your student, you will be able to look at a book and immediately know whether it is too hard or too easy for your student. Your judgment will then be better than any test or formula. Trust your instincts.

The Three Literacy Levels

LITSTART's "beginning level" is equivalent to the first-grade level, intermediate is second and third grade, and advanced is fourth through seventh grade; however, LITSTART avoids reference to grade levels other than this explanatory note. With a little practice, you will be able to identify the three literacy levels on sight by looking for general types of words and sentences as shown in the charts and samples below.

Types of Words in Each Level

Level	Types of Words	Syllables/Word
Beginning	Very short, simple, repetitive	mostly one
Intermediate	Short and simple	one or two
Advanced	Conversational, but not sophisticated	one to three

Types of Sentences in Each Level

Level	Sentence Style	Sentence Length
Beginning	Very short, unnatural sounding	4-8 words
Intermediate	More fluid, but still a little choppy	6-12 words
Advanced	Conversational	10-20 words

Comparative Samples of Each Reading Level

Beginning	I do not drive to work. I take the bus. I save money this way. I do not have to pay for gas. I do not have to pay for parking. I save money on gas. I save money on parking.
Intermediate	I don't drive my car to work. I take the bus instead. This saves me money because I don't pay for gas or parking. Parking is very high—five dollars a day. That would be twenty-five dollars a week!
Advanced	I could drive to work, but I decided to take the bus in order to save money. When I include the costs of parking, gas, and maintenance, I figure I must be saving a thousand dollars a year.

With a little practice, you will be able to identify the three literacy levels on sight.

*Walk
through the
activity in
your mind.*

Step 3: Select Strategies

You are now ready to put your priority topics and materials together into a plan for a tutoring session based on your student's abilities, interests, and goals. Follow these steps:

1. Assemble the following items:

    *   The Skills Checklist and Lesson Ideas (from pages 60-69) that match your student's ability level.
    *   Your priority topics from Step 1 (page 48).
    *   Your materials from Step 2 (page 49).
    *   A notebook to organize your notes.

2. Let's say you want to plan the reading part of the lesson first. On your Lesson Ideas page, find the suggested reading strategies. Examine those strategies in Chapter 6.

3. Select one or more reading strategies based on your student's needs and interests, your materials, and your own preference.

4. Prepare or read through the materials that you plan to use. Walk through the activity in your mind. Make any notes that will help you.

5. Repeat Steps 2, 3, and 4 above for the other parts of the lesson. Use the appropriate chapter below to help you plan each part:

    Speaking (ESL) .... Chapter 5
    Reading .... Chapter 6
    Word Study .... Chapter 7
    Writing .... Chapter 8

6. Think about a back-up plan in case you finish early or your first plan doesn't work out. (The Experience Story, Strategy 18, makes a good back-up plan for most students.) Make notes.

7. Think about homework (see next page). Make notes.

> **On pages 56-59 are samples
> of notes for tutoring sessions
> for two different students.**

~~Homework:~~ **Extra Practice at Home**

Homework is, of course, a good idea. However, avoid using the word "homework," which has juvenile connotations for some adults. Call it "practice," "extra work at home," or "extra spelling if you have time."

Some students will never do work at home—period. Others will do more than you ask. Your student, as an adult, must balance priorities just as you must. If studying doesn't make the list, just be glad for the time you have together and use it wisely.

Do not *assign* work for home. You can suggest it; you can encourage it; but do not *assign* it. Let your student decide how much work and what type of work to attempt at home.

Whatever work you suggest, make sure that it is relatively easy. Save the challenging work for your time together.

Here are some possible activities for work at home:

- Reread a story.
- Read a new story (not too difficult).
- Read with a family member, if appropriate.
- Review words that you have practiced together.
- Listen to tapes of sounds, words, or a reading.
- Listen to the news and watch TV (for ESL).
- Listen to radio, songs, or instructional tapes (for ESL).
- Speak English 10 minutes a day at home (for ESL).

Work is more likely to be done if the student can bring back something to show. The suggestions below meet that criterion.

- Answer written questions about a story that was read.
- Do workbook exercises.
- Practice spelling or penmanship.
- Copy words or sentences.
- Write in a journal.

If the student does work at home, be sure to review it at the next lesson. If the student "didn't have time," just say, "That's okay. Do you want to do it now together?"

Work is more likely to be done if the student can bring back something to show.

Tinh

Sample ESL Student: Tinh

Tinh is 27 and lives with his wife, three children, and parents. His goal is to be able to communicate in person and on the phone with his suppliers and his customers at his one-hour photo shop. According to *Where to Start,* Tinh functions on the ESL 2 level.

Planning Tinh's Lesson

Step 1: Select topics from the Master Topics List

Conversation ideas with priority topics for the day checked (✔):

    casual conversation (customers and neighbors)
✔ **parts of a camera**
✔ **problems with a photograph** (how to discuss)
    the development process
    problems with the development process
    prices
    making change
    checks and credit cards
    bounced checks
    photographic supplies
    children's activities (for talking to teachers)
    children's problems (for talking to teachers)

Step 2: Select materials (for priority topics checked above)

    sample photos and negatives from tutor's home
    camera from tutor's home
    old photography magazines from library give-away rack
    sample photos and negatives from Tinh's supplies
    camera from Tinh's supplies
    camera catalogs from Tinh's supplies

Step 3: Select strategies (see next page)

Sample Lesson for Tinh

1. SPEAKING

Focus for the day: <u>parts of a camera and talking to customers</u>

- *Make Picture Cards using old photography*
  magazines and Tinh's catalogs. Focus on: .... *Strategy 2*
        Parts of the camera
        Problems with pictures (bad color, focus...)
        Colors
- *Work with cards to build vocabulary* .... *Strategy 6*
        Parts of the camera
        Problems with pictures (bad color, focus...)
        Words for good pictures (clear, bright colors)
        Names of colors
- *Sentences and phrases* .... *Exercise C of Strategy 7*
        Pick a card and say a sentence or phrase.

- *Start phrase booklet of responses to customers*
  based on type of question or problem .... *Strategy 9*
- *Role play* .... *Strategy 13*
        Customers with questions about picture quality.

2. READING   *none today*

3. WORD STUDY   *none today*

4. WRITING   *none today*

Back-Up Plans   *Conversation (Strategy 8), more sight words or*
                word families, or harder exercises from Strategy 7

Extra Work at Home   *Review picture cards. Practice saying*
        sentences.

Sample Literacy Student: Clara

Clara, 54, lives alone and works as a custodian. She is widowed and has one son and two grandsons. Clara wants be able to read women's magazines and travel information. She hopes to travel when she retires. She also wants to be able to write letters that are "spelled right" to her grandchildren. According to *Where to Start*, Clara reads and spells on the intermediate level.

Lesson Planning

Step 1: Identify topics from the Master Topics List

Reading ideas with priority topics for the day checked (✔):
✔ **magazines**
✔ **travel information from library, newspaper, brochures**
  maps
  travel tips and guidebooks
  travelogues
  retirement preparation materials
  health tips?
  finance tips?
  general interest

Writing ideas with priority topics for the day checked (✔):
✔ **letters to grandchildren**
  pretend postcards from intended travel destinations
  letters to travel bureaus requesting information
  pretend travel journals

Step 2: Find materials for priority topics checked above

  magazines
  USA atlas
  USA picture book from library
  Book — *USA Travel*
  sampling of other travel books from library
  envelopes and stamps

Step 3: Select strategies (see next page)

Clara

Sample Lesson for Clara

1. READING

1. U.S. Atlas: ....Strategy 16
      3 columns - what do you know about USA and maps?
        - what do you want to know?
          Explain map skills as needed
        - what did you find out?

2. Book – USA Travel
    pre-reading - talk about photos, contents ...Strategy 14
      - vocab: continent, scenic, expensive, favorite
    reading - start Chapter 1 ....Strategies 21 & 22
      - watch for new vocab, comprehension, etc.
    post-reading: summary, reactions ....Strategy 22
      - would she like to go there? Why? Why not?
      - favorite part?
      - same book next time or different?

2. WORD STUDY

Word families - (select from reading as we go) ....Strategy 30
Spelling - word family words: -ide, -ight, -ime
      (Appendix E) ....Strategy 37

3. WRITING

Written Conversation ....Strategy 52
    If you could go anywhere in the world, ...
Everyday Scenario: Draft letter to granddaughter ..Strategy 51
    Then help her correct spelling.

Back-Up Plans
Extra Work at Home   Reread chapter in travel book.
                    Recopy letter to granddaughter.

ESL 1 Skills Checklist

If the student's goals are broad and general, use these two pages for ideas for skills to work on and for strategies to attain them. When these ESL 1 skills* have been attained, the student can move to ESL Level 2.

Speaking Skills

☐ Answers common greetings.

☐ Understands and uses critical nouns, such as names for common foods, tools used for work, family members, furniture, coins, and other words from the student's life.

☐ Understands and uses critical adjectives, such as good, big, hot, heavy, nice, old, and blue.

☐ Understands and uses critical verbs (present tense), such as come, go, buy, eat, work, drive, and words from the student's life.

☐ Can count to 100.

☐ Can convey basic ideas by stringing a few words together (although not grammatically accurate).

Reading Skills

(None)

Word Study Skills

☐ Recognizes numerals for 1 to 100 and the symbols $ and ¢.

☐ Recognizes the most important words from personal Picture Cards (Strategy 2) as sight words.

Writing Skills

☐ Can print own name from memory.

* These skills are intentionally stated loosely to discourage a formal testing atmosphere. Students should be able to perform the skills comfortably, consistently, without assistance, and with few errors.

ESL 1 – Lesson Ideas

The lesson ideas below illustrate how the broad goals on the preceding page can be met using strategies that are found in the next four chapters. If your student has more specific goals or needs, select only those strategies that meet your student's goals.

ESL Level 1

1. SPEAKING

- Practice common greetings *— and/or—*

- Practice important nouns using Strategies 1-3 *— and/or—*

- Practice basic adjectives using Strategy 3 or 5 *— and/or—*

- Practice basic verbs using Strategy 4 *— and/or—*

- Practice counting to 100 *— and/or—*

- Practice conveying basic ideas using Strategy 4 or 8.

2. READING

(None)

3. WORD STUDY

- Practice recognizing numerals and money symbols *— and/or—*

- Practice recognizing critical Picture Card words (Strategy 2) as sight words using Strategy 33.

4. WRITING

- Practice printing name.

Back-Up Plans	• Use catalog or picture dictionary to discuss words.
Extra Work at Home	• Watch TV, review notebook, copy words, review Picture Cards, or do workbook pages.

ESL 2 Skills Checklist

If the student's goals are broad and general, use these two pages for ideas for skills to work on and for strategies to attain them. When these ESL 2 skills* have been attained, the student can move to the beginning literacy level.

Speaking Skills

☐ Knows everyday nouns, such as the names of job-related items, foods, clothing, toiletries, body parts, appliances, kitchenware, vehicles, local landmarks, and other items from the student's life.

☐ Knows everyday adjectives describing such characteristics as size, shape, quality, composition, and appearance.

☐ Knows the present form of everyday verbs.

☐ Is beginning to use the past, present, and future forms of verbs (including irregular past forms such as *went* and *saw).*

☐ Communicates simple ideas in fairly complete sentences (one or two words may be incorrect and pronunciation may be inaccurate).

☐ Communicates with co-workers, store clerks, and bank tellers well enough to manage routine affairs with minimal assistance.

Reading Skills

☐ Can read own half-page Experience Story (Strategy 18).

Word Study Skills

☐ Can identify the letters of the alphabet, capital or small, at random.

☐ Recognizes most words from Picture Cards.

☐ Can write a few critical words from memory.

Writing Skills

☐ Can print all the letters, both capital and small, at random.

☐ Can print name and full address from memory.

* These skills are intentionally stated loosely to discourage a formal testing atmosphere. Students should be able to perform the skills comfortably, consistently, without assistance, and with few errors.

ESL 2 – Lesson Ideas

The lesson ideas below illustrate how the broad goals on the preceding page can be met using strategies that are found in the next four chapters. If your student has more specific goals or needs, select only those strategies that meet your student's goals.

ESL Level 2

1. SPEAKING

- Practice everyday nouns using Strategies 6, 7, 9 — *and/or*—
- Practice adjectives using Strategies 5, 6, 9, 11 — *and/or*—
- Practice everyday verbs and their tenses using Strategies 4, 6, 11, 12 — *and/or*—
- Practice communicating in complete sentences using Strategies 4-13.

2. READING

- Do an Experience Story (Strategy 18).

3. WORD STUDY

- Practice identifying the letters of the alphabet using Strategy 26 — *and/or*—
- Practice recognizing words from Experience Story and Picture Cards using Strategy 33 — *and/or*—
- Practice writing critical sight words using Strategy 39 or 40.

4. WRITING

- Practice printing if not legible — *and/or*—
- Practice printing name and full address.

Back-Up Plans
- Experience Story (Strategy 18); catalog or picture dictionary as source of conversation (Strategy 8)

Extra Work at Home
- Watch TV, copy words, do workbook pages, copy Experience Story, or review notebook.

Beginning Literacy Skills Checklist

If the student's goals are broad and general, use these two pages for ideas for skills to work on and for strategies to attain them. When these beginning skills* have been attained, the student can move to the intermediate literacy level.

Reading Skills

☐ Can read most beginning-level material (see page 53) with comprehension.

☐ Can read own one-page Experience Stories (Strategy 18).

Word Study Skills

☐ Can identify the letters of the alphabet, capital or small, at random.

☐ Can identify the initial consonant sounds of most words from Appendix A read by a tutor at random.

☐ (optional) Recognizes the short vowel sounds (pages 132-133).

☐ Can **read** most words in random order from:

    ☐ the Beginning Sight Word list in Appendix K.

    ☐ the Beginning Word Families lists in Appendix E.

☐ Can **spell** most words from the Beginning Word Families lists in Appendix E.

Writing Skills

☐ Can print all the letters, both capital and small.

☐ Can print name and full address from memory.

☐ Can write and read a short shopping list using Strategy 51.

☐ Can complete Beginning Guided Writing exercises (Strategy 53).

☐ Can write simple dictated sentences using beginning word-family words, periods, and capital letters (Strategy 55).

---

* These skills are intentionally stated loosely to discourage a formal testing atmosphere. Students should be able to perform the skills comfortably, consistently, without assistance, and with few errors (except for the temporary spelling inherent in Strategy 51).

Beginning Literacy – Lesson Ideas

The lesson ideas below illustrate how the broad goals on the preceding page can be met using strategies that are found in Chapters 6, 7, and 8. If your student has more specific goals or needs, select only those strategies that meet your student's goals.

Beginning Literacy Level

1. READING

- Do an Experience Story (Strategy 18) — *and/or—*

- Read from the student's selected easy reading material using Strategies 14, 21, and 22 — *and/or—*

- Read more difficult material using Strategy 15 or 17 for pre-reading and/or Strategy 19 or 20 for during-reading — *and/or—*

- If comprehension needs work, break the reading into smaller segments and use Strategies 14 and 22 more intensely.

2. WORD STUDY

- Work on one of the following:
  Initial consonant sounds, using Strategies 26, 27
  Beginning word families, using Strategies 30, 31, 32
  Beginning sight words, using Strategy 33 — *and/or—*

- Practice spelling word family patterns, using Strategies 36 and 37.

3. WRITING

- Practice printing if not legible — *and/or—*

- Practice writing name and full address from memory — *and/or—*

- Practice writing lists using Strategy 51 — *and/or—*

- Practice Beginning Guided Writing (Strategy 53) — *and/or—*

- Practice simple Dictated Sentences (Strategy 55).

Back-Up Plans • Experience Story (Strategy 18)

Extra Work at Home • Copy words, do workbook pages, or reread stories.

Intermediate Literacy Skills Checklist

If the student's goals are broad and general, use these two pages for ideas for target skills and tutoring strategies. When these intermediate skills* have been attained, the student can move to the advanced literacy level.

Reading Skills

- ☐ Can read most intermediate-level material (see page 53) with comprehension.
- ☐ Can read own Experience Stories (Strategy 18) three pages long.

Word Study Skills

- ☐ (optional) Recognizes long, short, and other vowel sounds and the cues for them (pages 132-133).
- ☐ Recognizes the sounds of blends and digraphs (pages 130-131).
- ☐ Can **read** most words at random from:
    - ☐ The Intermediate Word Families lists in Appendices E and F.
    - ☐ The Intermediate Sight Word list in Appendix K.
- ☐ Can **spell** most words at random from:
    - ☐ The Intermediate Word Families lists in Appendices E and F.
    - ☐ The above word family words with the endings -S, -ED, -ING, -ER, and -EST (see pages 136-137).
    - ☐ The Beginning (not Intermediate) Sight Word list in Appendix K.
- ☐ Can read and interpret contractions in Appendix J.

Writing Skills

- ☐ Uses temporary spelling as needed (Strategy 50).
- ☐ Uses writing for at least three everyday situations.
- ☐ Can write conversational thoughts that others can understand.
- ☐ Can write a coordinated paragraph of at least three sentences.
- ☐ Can write simple dictated sentences using intermediate words, periods, question marks, and capital letters.
- ☐ (optional) Can write legibly in cursive (see page 173).

* These skills are intentionally stated loosely to discourage a formal testing atmosphere. Students should be able to perform the skills comfortably, consistently, without assistance, and with few errors.

Intermediate Level – Lesson Ideas

The lesson ideas below demonstrate how the broad goals on the preceding page can be met using strategies that are found in Chapters 6, 7, and 8. If your student has more specific goals or needs, select only those strategies that meet your student's goals.

Intermediate Literacy Level

1. READING

- Do an Experience Story (Strategy 18) — *and/or*—

- Read from the selected intermediate reading material using Strategies 14, 21, and 22. Add Strategy 16, 23, 24, or 25 for extra work on comprehension — *and/or*—

- Read more difficult material using Strategy 15 or 17 for pre-reading and/or Strategy 19 or 20 for during-reading.

2. WORD STUDY

- Work on one of the following:
    Sounds of blends, digraphs, or vowels, using
        Strategy 26, 27, 28, 29, 32, 34, or 36.
    Intermediate Word Families, using Strategies 30-32
    Intermediate Sight Words, using Strategy 33
    Contractions, using Strategy 12 — *and/or*—

- Practice spelling word family patterns and endings using Strategies 37 and 38 — *and/or*—

- Practice spelling Beginning (not Intermediate) Sight Words using Strategy 39, 40, 41, or 42

3. WRITING

- Practice writing for everyday situations (Strategy 51) — *and/or*—

- Practice writing conversational thoughts using Strategy 52 or 58 or both — *and/or*—

- Practice writing paragraphs using Strategy 54 or 57 or both — *and/or*—

- Practice Dictated Sentences (Strategy 55).

Back-Up Plans
- Experience Story (Strategy 18), or read from another book.

Extra Work at Home
- Write journal; do workbook; reread story.

Advanced Literacy Skills Checklist

If the student's goals are broad and general, use these two pages for ideas for skills to work on and for strategies to attain them. When these advanced skills* have been attained, the student can graduate from the literacy program and move on to another program in your community.

Reading Skills

☐ Can read advanced level material (see page 53) with comprehension.

Word Study Skills

☐ Can read:

   ☐ Most of the long words in Appendices G and H.

   ☐ All Advanced Sight Words in Appendix K at random.

☐ Recognizes and uses prefixes UN-, DIS-, PRE-, and RE-, and suffixes -TION, -SION, and -LY to figure out new words.

☐ Can find a given word in the dictionary.

☐ Can **spell** most words from:

   ☐ The long words in Appendices G and H.

   ☐ The Intermediate and Advanced Sight Word lists in Appendix K.

   ☐ The contractions in Appendix J.

Writing Skills

☐ Uses temporary spelling as needed (Strategy 50).

☐ Uses writing routinely for everyday situations.

☐ Can comfortably write two pages of conversational thoughts that are easy for others to read.

☐ Has tried Guided Writing; Writing 1, 2, 3; and Free Writing (and word processing on a computer) several times each.

☐ Can write stories, letters, or reports of at least five paragraphs using Process Writing with assistance on Steps 3 and 4.

* These skills are intentionally stated loosely to discourage a formal testing atmosphere. Students should be able to perform the skills comfortably, consistently, without assistance, and with few errors.

Advanced Level – Lesson Ideas

The lesson ideas below demonstrate how the broad goals on the preceding page can be met using strategies that are found in Chapters 6, 7, and 8. If your student has more specific goals or needs, select only those strategies that meet your student's goals.

*Advanced
Literacy Level*

1. READING

- Read advanced reading material using Strategies 14, 21, and 22; add Strategy 16, 23, 24, or 25 for extra work on comprehension — *and/or* —

- Read difficult material using Strategy 15 or 17.

2. WORD STUDY

- Practice reading long words using Strategies 44 through 49 in sequence — *and/or* —

- Practice reading Advanced Sight Words (Appendix K) — *and/or* —

- Practice spelling long words using Strategy 38 — *and/or* —

- Practice spelling Intermediate and Advanced Sight Words and contractions using Strategy 39, 40, 41, or 42.

3. WRITING

- Practice writing for everyday situations (Strategy 51) — *and/or* —

- Practice writing conversational thoughts using Strategy 52 or 58 or both — *and/or* —

- Practice Guided Writing (Strategy 54); Writing 1, 2, 3 (Strategy 57); Free Writing (Strategy 59); or word processing — *and/or* —

- Practice writing stories, letters, or reports using Process Writing (Strategy 60).

Back-Up Plans • Read from another book.

Extra Work at Home • Write in journal (Strategy 58), do workbook pages, or read a section and answer questions.

Later Sessions

As you work with your student, you will gradually learn what works and what doesn't work for your student.

Most of the tutoring strategies in Chapters 5, 6, 7, and 8 are appropriate for most students, but some can be especially useful for certain situations. If a strategy works well for you and your student, use it again. If a strategy does not work, modify it or discard it. If you think of a new strategy, do what good teachers do: try it.

Periodically review and revise your Master Topics List from Step 1 in this chapter. Use it for ideas to build later lessons.

Remember:

- What works for one tutor/student pair may not work for the next.

- Don't be afraid to experiment.

- Your student is the best judge of what works. Ask for feedback: Did this make sense? Which way is better? Which would you rather do?

5 Speaking

"I can no speak doctor, neighbor, teacher. I have no American friends. No speak good"

—Li-Ying, an ESL student

Speaking

This chapter will provide tips for working with ESL students and will present 13 strategies for teaching ESL students to speak English:

Students Learning to Speak English

Students who grew up speaking any language other than English are known as ESL (English as a Second Language) students. For them, English is a foreign language.

Most people learn their first language in a logical progression:

> Hear it ⇒ Speak it ⇒ Read it ⇒ Write it

As they progress to each new step, they continue to build their earlier skills. For example, as they learn to read, they continue to improve their abilities to understand and to speak the language.

This same progression—hear, speak, read, write—is logical for acquiring a second language. In fact, however, many ESL students can read English better than they can speak it. For such students, reading can be an extra tool, but it can also be a crutch.

This chapter covers only the speaking component of working with ESL students. ("Speaking" here means hearing, understanding, and speaking—ultimately without notes.) Reading and other parts of the ESL lesson are explained in later chapters.

Many ESL students can read English better than they can speak it.

	RECEIVING MESSAGES	SENDING MESSAGES
ORAL MESSAGES	HEAR AND UNDERSTAND	SPEAK
WRITTEN MESSAGES	READ AND UNDERSTAND	WRITE

ESL Levels

ESL students are divided into ESL Level 1, ESL Level 2, and higher levels of ESL, which merge with literacy instruction. For a more detailed description of ESL levels, see pages 36-39.

Communicating with Your Student

Many ESL students already know at least a little English. However, the less English your student knows, the more you will need the guidelines below.

- Stick to simple, important messages.

- Speak at a relaxed pace, but not unnaturally slow.

- Choose simple, common words. Say "very big" rather than "huge."

- Speak in normal, complete sentences. Say "Did you go to the store?" not "You go store?" even if your student doesn't understand all the words.

- Enunciate clearly but not unnaturally.

- Listen to your student. Watch for patterns in your student's errors so that you can address them in future lessons.

- If you don't understand something your student says, say so. Try again. Work it out.

- Try repeating or paraphrasing your student's words.

- Do not make the mistake of talking loudly as if that will help the person understand you better.

- Use diagrams and sketches. If you can't draw well, draw poorly and laugh about it.

- Use facial expressions, pantomiming, role playing, models, pictures, or any means you can think of to communicate.

- Relax and take your time. Keep repeating.

- Smile!

Stick to simple, important messages.

Additional ESL Tips

- Collect pictures from magazines, newspapers, catalogs (lots of pictures of lots of things), and advertisements. Store them in folders by topic. They will facilitate some wonderful interaction!

- Check often to make sure the student truly understands you. Some ESL students nod and say yes just to be polite. Ask the student to restate or explain things back to you.

- Try to teach words in phrases or sentences rather than in isolation. Teach "What time is it?" as a unit, not as four separate words.

- Teach idioms just as you would new vocabulary. English has thousands of expressions or idioms that make little sense when the words are translated literally. You might "run out of" soap but you weren't running. A few other examples are: "he *caught* a cold" or "she *ran into* an old friend" or "they *burst out* laughing" or "don't *beat around the bush*." You'll be amazed at how often you use idioms.

- Limit the amount of information you provide about a topic. For example, when introducing numbers, don't explain the difference between *two*, *too* and *to*. Stay within one context. Think of the topic as a folder that contains only information that should be filed together. Open only one folder at a time.

- Define words by using your own explanation and examples. Save dictionaries for advanced literacy students.

- Do not use a dictionary that has both the student's native language and English except as a last resort. (Dictionaries detract from conversation opportunities and sometimes give definitions that are hard to understand.) Talk instead.

- Review the tips on pages 8-11. They apply just as much to ESL students as to literacy students.

Some ESL students nod and say yes just to be polite.

Grammar and Pronunciation

It is common for sentences spoken by ESL students to contain multiple errors in grammar and pronunciation. If you correct every error, not only will you both become quickly discouraged, but you will devalue the message that your student is trying to communicate.

Error is part of the learning process. Since your student will outgrow many errors automatically with experience, the best way to help is often to ignore minor errors and just continue conversing.

Corrections During Conversation

If your student says to you, "Sorry late; baby sick," your response should be not to correct the verbs, but to ask about the baby. Then you can discuss symptoms, thermometers, doctors, and prescriptions. Correct the grammar or pronunciation only as needed to clarify the message or if your student asks.

Often you can repeat some or all of the student's words in your response. "Your baby is sick? I'm so sorry. What is wrong?" In this way you demonstrate the correct pronunciation and grammar without demeaning the message. Your student will note the corrections either consciously or subconsciously. Either way, your words add to the data that the student's brain is sorting and processing. Your words supply the clues.

Corrections During Structured Exercise

As the student progresses, you might notice a consistent grammatical problem, such as plurals or past tense, that you can practice with your student in a structured exercise such as Strategy 12. Focus on that one issue for several sessions until it's mastered. Correcting several unrelated errors at one time may be overwhelming.

If you correct every error, you will devalue your student's message.

Cultural Issues

Your student's culture is undoubtedly different from yours. While many differences can spark interesting conversation, other differences, especially regarding body positions, may cause misunderstandings. Here are a few guidelines:

- *Be overly polite and respectful at first*. Resist the American tendency to be instant pals. Give your student a little time.

- *Invite your student to call you by your first name*, but don't insist. Your student may be uncomfortable with anything but "Ms. Doe." Sometimes "Ms. Jane" can be a compromise. Ask how your student wishes to be addressed.

- *Use a pen or use your entire hand, open palm, to point.* Pointing, especially with certain fingers, is rude in some cultures.

- *Avoid gestures.* Your "thumbs up" or a circle "okay" sign might mean something different, perhaps even offensive, in your student's culture.

- *Provide the student with a person-free comfort zone.* Don't crowd the student, and don't touch the student. Even the most innocent touch on the arm may be misinterpreted.

- *Watch for cues from your student*. For example, if the student doesn't look you in the eye, then minimize eye contact. If the student sits far away, then respect that personal space. If your student points, then pointing is okay. Notice which finger your student uses.

- *Provide cultural experiences.* Take the bus downtown; walk to the park; carve a pumpkin. Talk about it as you go.

- *Show interest in and respect for your student's culture.* Ask your student about customs and behaviors. Perhaps your library can also provide information.

- *Talk about holidays.* National and religious holidays that you take for granted may be new to your student. Likewise, your student may celebrate holidays that you don't. Share your cultures by discussing holidays as they happen. If you discuss religion, do it in an objective manner.

The amount of formal education that students have had in their native languages affects your tutoring.

ESL Student Backgrounds

The amount of formal education that ESL students have had in their native languages and the amount of informal exposure that students have had to English affects your work as a tutor.

Students who are well educated in their native language

These students know how to study. They often seem to read better than they speak (either because of good phonics skills or because of previous English instruction that focused on reading). Such students take lots of notes and are inclined to speak phonetically, pronouncing the word *liked*, for example, as *"like Ed."*

Encourage these students to set their pens aside, at least some of the time, and just converse with you. Explain that this is practice for real life, when they won't always have their notes handy. How you divide your lesson time between speaking skills and literacy skills will depend on the student's own goals and preferences.

Students with little formal education

These students are probably weak not only in literacy skills in their native language, but in basic social studies, science, and arithmetic concepts as well. They may have little experience in being a student.

Focus first on speaking skills and gradually progress to reading and writing. Proceed slowly and check comprehension frequently. Have simple maps and a picture dictionary handy to help explain new concepts that may arise. You may want to show the student how to study and how to organize information.

Students who already speak fairly well but can't read or write may have learned English on their own from television and work. Such students are probably fairly comfortable with the culture.

Focus on reading and writing rather than speaking. Vocabulary and grammar will improve automatically as a result of your literacy instruction.

New Nouns   *Strategy 1* ////////

Uses: To introduce new nouns to ESL Level 1 students.

Materials: Items and pictures of items important for the student to know

Procedure: 1. Introduce an item. "This is a table." Repeat.

2. Ask "What is this?" Expect only a one-word answer. Help if needed.

3. Discuss a second item using the same process.

4. After the student learns the second noun, review both nouns by asking "What is this?" several times.

5. Add a few more nouns and review in random order. (Review the 85% Rule on page 10 for guidance on how many nouns to introduce.)

––––––––––––––––––––––––––––––––

6. At later lessons, review old nouns and add new ones.

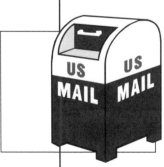

Strategy 2 Picture Cards — Basic

Uses: To create a permanent study collection of the ESL Level 1 student's important words.

Materials: Cards; scissors; glue; and pictures from magazines, catalogs, ads, newspapers, or work (focus on one area such as money, kitchen utensils, job tools, numbers, food, family members, shapes, colors, vehicles, or animals)

Procedure:

1. Using simple sentences, discuss items in the pictures, constantly explaining, describing, and asking the student to repeat.

2. Working together, select, cut out, and glue important pictures on separate cards, constantly talking.

3. On the back of the card, help the student write the English word for the picture. Invite your student, if sufficiently literate, to make other notes in English or in the student's native language.

4. Review the cards at random and save for Strategies 3, 5, 6, 7, and 33.

5. Encourage the student to keep the cards in a pocket in the student's notebook (page 9) and to study the cards at home.

---

6. At later lessons, review the cards and add more.

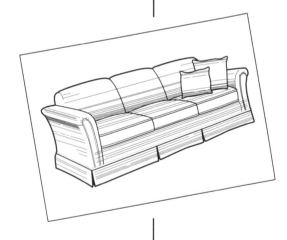

Card Games — Basic

Strategy 3 ///////

Uses: To practice words with ESL 1 students.

Materials: Picture Cards (Strategy 2), pictures, or objects that are related and important to the student

Procedure: **A. EASIEST**

1. Scatter the pictures or items on the table.

2. Say, "Please find the spoon." Demonstrate if the student doesn't understand.

3. Ask the student to repeat the word.

4. If the answer is correct, set the picture aside.

B. HARDER

Guide the student in sorting selected cards or items according to use, color, size, shape, appearance, or other characteristics. Discuss as you sort.

See also harder card games in Strategy 7.

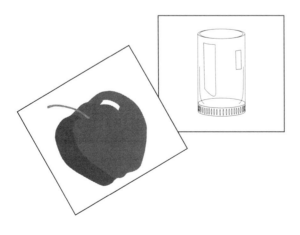

Sanilac District Library

Strategy 4 — Moving

look at

take

eat

wash

open

put

turn

go

come

laugh

sleep

walk

lose

talk to

drive

Uses: To practice verbs and related phrases, especially for ESL Level 1 students who learn kinesthetically.

Materials: Familiar objects that are important to the student

Procedure:
1. Perform an action while you describe it. "I pick up the pen." Repeat several times.

2. Gesture (open palm) to your student to repeat your action and words several times.

3. Say, "Please pick up the pen." Avoid looking at the item or giving other clues unless needed.

4. Reverse roles. Touch the pen as a cue and gesture for your student to ask you to "please pick up the pen." (Be sure to comply!)

5. Add more actions, one at a time, using Steps 1 and 2 to introduce the action and Steps 3 and 4 to practice it. "I look at the clock." "I open the book." For Steps 3 and 4, randomly mix the new action several times with other actions you have practiced.

6. If the student can read, help the student create a list of the new words for the student's notebook (page 9).

---

7. At future lessons, add new actions and continue to review the old actions.

Describe an Object

Strategy 5 /////////

Uses: To add adjectives to the student's vocabulary.

Materials: A collection of objects, pictures, and Picture Cards (Strategy 2) the student knows

Procedure:
1. Review a few items: "This is a pen. This is a marker. This is a piece of paper."

2. Add a color. "This is a red pen." Explain the meaning. Repeat with other items. "This is a red hat."

3. Ask the student to repeat the new sentences. Review until the student knows the words.

4. Introduce related adjectives. "This is a blue pen."

5. Ask the student to find objects. "Where's the blue pen?" Ask for a verbal answer. "Here is the blue pen."

6. Ask the student to describe objects. "What color is this pen?" Expect only a one-word response.

_____

7. At later sessions, review and add new items. Also add new adjectives to describe shape, size, texture, composition, number, appearance, or other characteristics.

_____

8. For intermediate students, try multiple adjectives ("two shiny black pens").

three

small

old

green

shiny

short

bad

clean

cold

nice

funny

soft

Strategy 6

Picture Cards — Enhanced

Uses: To build vocabulary (adjectives, verbs, nouns, and prepositions) for ESL Level 2 using the student's important nouns as a base.

Materials: Picture Cards (Strategy 2)

Procedure:
1. Ask the student to select a card.

2. Discuss the item in detail, introducing related verbs and adjectives. ("This chair is a folding chair. The chair is made of metal. I sat in the chair yesterday.") Ask the student to repeat each sentence after you.

3. Ask the student questions. "What kind of chair is this?" "What is the chair made of?"

4. Encourage the student to select important words, phrases, or sentences from Step 2 and add those words to the card.

5. Continue with other cards.

___

6. At later sessions, review and add new items.

Cup

coffee cup
cup of tea
hot cup of coffee
cup and saucer

Card Games — Enhanced

Strategy 7 ///////////

Uses: To practice words and sentences with ESL Level 2 students.

Materials: Objects, pictures, and Picture Cards (Strategy 2) that are related and important to the student

Procedure: **C. HARD** (compare to Strategy 3)

1. Ask the student to pick an item and say the word (and perhaps develop a phrase or sentence for each word).

2. If the answer is correct, set the item aside; if not, return it to the original pile.

D. HARDER

1. Scatter the items on the table.

2. Give a clue: "Can you find a vegetable," or "Please find a thing to use for writing."

3. Encourage the student to respond with a sentence. "This is a carrot."

E. HARDEST

1. Ask the student to select two cards without looking.

2. Help the student to make up a sentence that uses both words and, if possible, place the objects or perform the action described by the sentence. "The spoon is on the chair."

See also easier card games in Strategy 3.

Strategy 8   Conversation

Uses: To practice conversation, increase vocabulary, and explore real-life situations.

Procedure: 1. Start a conversation about any topic of interest to your student. Discuss families, jobs, pets, chores. (Also, be prepared at any time to set aside your planned lesson and discuss any topic that your student brings up.) Did something happen in the news? Did something happen in your student's life? All conversation is helpful to your student.

2. Discuss the event or situation. Use role playing, diagrams, sketches, or whatever works. Answer your student's questions.

3. Consider using the topic as a page in your student's notebook (page 9) or as an Experience Story (Strategy 18). Consider using words from the conversation as the basis for Strategy 4, 6, 7, 9, 11, 12, or 13.

Focus Booklets

Strategy 9

Uses: To collect and organize critical words and phrases for the student's reference at work or for errands.

Materials: Pictures, small notebook(s), glue or tape, scissors, (optional: colored markers)

Procedure:

1. With the student, collect or draw pictures from **one** topic area important to the student (such as food, clothing, work, money, baby care, emergencies, colors, shapes, furniture, or family members). Discuss as you work. Divide the pictures into groups (vegetables, fruit, dairy).

2. Help the student glue a picture or two on each page.

3. Work together to add labels, descriptive words, arrows, explanations, or sample sentences. Notes can be made in the student's native language.

4. Discuss as you work. Use the words in sentences and have the student repeat. Ask questions.

5. Encourage the student to take this booklet to work or on errands to use as a reference. At other times, it can be stored in a pocket of the student's notebook.

6. At future lessons, review the booklet and add words or make additional booklets focused on other topics.

Strategy 10 — Field Trips

Bank

Hardware store

Grocery store

Department store

Post office

Park

Mall

Medical center

City hall

Museum

School

Local landmarks

Library

Bus station

Employment office

Uses: To increase vocabulary, practice speaking, and study culture in a real-life setting based on the student's needs.

Materials: Map, pictures of methods of transportation, pictures of anticipated activities and items

Procedure:

1. Together, find the departure point and destination on the map. Help the student practice sentences. "We are going to the hardware store." "The hardware store is on Fourth Avenue."

2. Using pictures, discuss transportation and probable sights and activities. Practice sentences. Create a section in the student's notebook for sketches and notes.

3. Discuss and practice useful sentences and write them down. "How much does it cost?"

4. Take the trip with the student. Discuss activities and sights along the way and at the site. Help the student write down new words.

5. After the trip, discuss the trip and new words.

---

6. At later lessons, review the notes and expand on new words using Strategies 6, 7, 8, 9, and 13.

—Lines of Progression—

Strategy 11

Uses:　To teach verb tenses or degrees of words such as love——hate, wonderful——terrible, or cold——hot.

Procedure:

1. While discussing the selected concept, draw a line and label three or more points along the line.

—X————————X————————X—
　Yesterday　　Today　　Tomorrow
　drove　　　　drive　　will drive

2. Demonstrate the concept with a few sentences. (Point to "today," pretend to drive, and say "I drive my car." Point to yesterday. "I drove my car yesterday.")

3. Supply questions to help your student practice the words at random. "What did I do yesterday?"

4. Help your student copy the verb tenses line from Step 1 above into the student's notebook (page 9) and start a list of action words with past, present, and future forms. (Regular verbs [those that just add -ED] and irregular verbs [such as go/went, eat/ate, and do/did] could be put on separate pages.)

X————X————X
Tall　　Taller　　Tallest

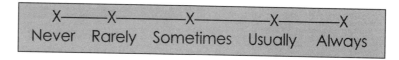

X————X————X————X————X
Never　Rarely　Sometimes　Usually　Always

Strategy 12 Language Patterns

Uses:
To practice patterns or exceptions in the language (such as plurals, negatives, questions, pronouns, contractions, and verb tenses).

Materials:
Lists of words and examples you have carefully thought out or researched ahead of time (use only consistent samples first; teach the exceptions later)

Procedure:
1. Explain to the student the skill that you want to practice. (Avoid grammatical terms.)

2. Illustrate the skill with several examples. Ask the student to repeat the words after you. If appropriate, add a chart and help the student copy the chart into the student's notebook.

3. Help the student practice the skill by changing sentences you supply.

   For example, to show plurals, you could say, "I have an apple." Your student would respond, "I have *two apples*." For negatives, it could be "Kim works here" and "Kim *doesn't work* here." Offer 10 or 20 practice sentences.

Note: Often changing a sentence involves altering two or three words. Many changes, such as the -S on the end of the verb, are subtle. That is why it is important to start with simple, consistent examples and to select your examples carefully.

Role Playing   *Strategy 13*

Uses: To increase vocabulary and practice communicating in a scenario based on the student's needs.

Materials: Props, if needed, depending on the scenario

Procedure: 1. Together, decide the scenario you will practice based on situations the student has encountered or is likely to encounter.

2. If the student wishes, write out a script or key phrases first. (Alternatively, you might experiment and practice first and write a script afterwards.)

3. Let the student take the role that is easier or the role that is closer to the student's real life.

4. If possible, "greet" your student or otherwise supply the first line or cue to start the activity. Try to stay in character even if your student has difficulty.

5. After the dialogue, compliment the student on communicating successfully. Point out some effective phrases that the student used. Then make just one or two suggestions for improvement.

6. If the student wishes, repeat the scenario the same way, with a new twist, or perhaps in opposite roles.

- *cashing a check at the bank*

- *explaining a problem to the landlord*

- *asking the boss for a day off*

- *asking a store clerk for help*

- *talking to a child's teacher*

6 Reading

"You don't notice right away that you are learning to read. It's sneaky. First you see a bunch of words you don't know. Then suddenly, it's like a light goes on in your head."

---James, an adult literacy student

Reading

This chapter will provide you with information about reading instruction and with 12 strategies for teaching reading:

The Reading Part of the Lesson

The reading part of the lesson consists of simply reading and enjoying written material with your student.

Reading is not phonics, workbooks, word lists, or flash cards. Reading means sentences, paragraphs, stories, and information. Reading means reading.

As explained in Chapter 4, the reading matter for the lesson can be anything from a medicine bottle or a recipe to a newspaper, a textbook, or a novel. The reading material should be based on the student's interests and needs.

Reading instruction may expand into other subjects if your student lacks the background knowledge to understand the reading material. If your student doesn't know where Africa is, get out the atlas. If your student doesn't know why Abraham Lincoln is famous or how to measure a tablespoon or why recycling saves trees, explain it. If you don't know the answer yourself, just say so and look it up— either later or on the spot.

If you have enough time, you might consider having two reading activities. For example, you could read from the newspaper at the beginning of the session and then from a favorite book at the end.

The Essence of Reading

> *Comprehension*
> *is the essence of reading;*
> *without comprehension,*
> *reading does not occur.*

Some experts have said that reading is the process of finding the meaning in a selection of print and that it takes three elements—the reader, the text, and the context—coming together to make reading happen.

Reader: The reader brings many elements to the table:

- Motivation to read
- Prior knowledge of the subject matter
- Understanding of the vocabulary and patterns of the language
- Reading skills, such as the ability to recognize some words and to figure out other words

Text: The writer brings the content and the language.

The publisher brings the size of the type, the layout, the pictures, other graphics, and the "feel" of the book.

Context: The environment also affects the reading.

- The purpose for reading (pleasure? interest? need? assignment?) affects the reader's level of concentration and intensity. It affects whether the reader reads for detail or for general impressions.
- The physical environment (lighting, temperature, noise level) may hamper or enhance the reader's ability to concentrate.

What Is It Like?

What is it like to have trouble with reading? Most of us have been reading for so long that it is hard to remember.

While it is impossible to recreate the total experience of illiteracy, the following exercise might provide some insight. Start at the star and read right to left instead of left to right. As you read, observe yourself. Notice how your brain works.

Backwards Reading Exercise

✱ Mark and Cynthia live on a little lake in the city. The lake has two paths that go all the way around it. One path is for walkers and the other path is for people on bicycles or roller blades. It is three miles around the lake.

Every day when the weather is nice, the paths are crowded with people walking, jogging, and biking. Cynthia gets up early every morning and jogs around the lake before breakfast no matter what the weather is. Mark doesn't jog, but he likes to stroll part way around and then come back.

At one end of the lake is a rose garden and a boat rental facility. At the other end is a band shell and a playground for the kids. As you can guess, Mark and Cynthia feel very lucky to live on such a nice lake.

How did you feel? How would you describe your reading? Which words gave you trouble? What did you do when you had trouble with a word? What kind of help would you have wanted, if any? How was your comprehension?

Give some thought to these questions before turning the page. What are the implications of your answers for tutoring?

Results of the Backwards Reading Exercise

In the exercise on the previous page, you may have noticed one or more of these occurrences:

- feelings of frustration or tension
- feelings of motivation and pride
- a choppy, hesitant reading style
- eyestrain (perhaps even a headache)
- mistaking letters (*b* for *d*) or words (*live* for *evil*)
- a desire for larger type or different style of type
- using the context to help with words like "on the l___"
- more trouble at the beginning of a sentence when you had no context
- skipping a tricky word, reading to the end of the sentence, and then coming back
- spelling a word letter-by-letter to figure it out
- poor recall of the story content
- a need for a break after just a few minutes

These are all characteristics and strategies of beginning readers. It is good to be aware of the emotions and physical effects that reading might have on your student.

Implications for tutoring:

- Be patient.
- Give encouragement; acknowledge successes.
- Try to use large, clear type.
- Don't worry about letter and word reversals for early readers. Reversals are a natural stage of learning to read.
- When the student hesitates on a word, wait a few moments before supplying help.
- If help is needed, just supply the word.
- Ask questions to help the student focus on the content.
- Give frequent mini-breaks (just pausing to discuss the reading serves as a break for the eyes and the processing part of the brain).

Comprehension Myths

Myth #1
Students must know the words or be able to sound out words before reading the text.

Not necessarily. Try this:

> Here are some words that you cannot sound out:

> mxxxxxn,   hixx,   yxxxx

> Now try them in context:

> Almxxx evxxx yxxr, Mrs. Crooks climbs up
> a <u>mxxxxxn</u> whxch is ovxx fourtxxx
> thxxxxxx fxxt <u>hixx</u>. Mrs. Crooks xx ninexx-
> one <u>yxxxx</u> old.

Reading is not just knowing the words and then comprehending; reading is also comprehending and then knowing the words.

Implications for tutoring:

Comprehension, awareness of language patterns, and prior knowledge (in this case prior knowledge about mountains, height, and age) all contribute to the reader's ability to figure out words. Reading is not just knowing the words and then comprehending; reading is also comprehending and then knowing the words.

Help the student integrate comprehension with word recognition to make reading a dynamic process. Use questions like:

- Does that make sense? Let's read it again.
- What word would make sense in that spot?
- Let's skip that word and read the rest of the sentence. Maybe then we will have an idea of what the word is.

These are techniques that good readers use when they encounter unknown words (as you do when you see a foreign phrase in a text).

Myth #2:
Students who recognize and understand all the words comprehend the text.

Not necessarily. Try this:

> They had a purple miracle for three bloated rocks. A man with a tasty highway will open the night for the April maple. If ever a dog needed a flaming song, this grassy table will tell me today.

Now explain what it means.

Implications for tutoring:

Obviously, the passage means nothing. But it does illustrate that it is possible to understand each word and yet not understand the passage. New readers often focus so intently on figuring out each word that they lose the overall meaning. (Some ESL students, in particular, pronounce many more words than they understand.)

It may be easy for you, listening to the student clearly pronounce all the words, to assume that the student understands the material as well as you do. Make no such assumption. **Ask questions** to determine how much the student understands—even if the text seems very simple. Students who anticipate that their tutors will ask questions soon learn to pay attention to the meaning as they read.

Myth #3
Students who can answer questions comprehend the text.

Not necessarily. Try this:

> Jan bought a new stecker at the hardware store. She needed a stecker for her minkle. Everybody knows that a minkle won't dreep if doesn't have a good stecker.
>
> ---
>
> What did Jan buy?
>
> What did she need it for?
>
> What would have happened if Jan hadn't bought it?

Implications for tutoring:

Clearly, it is possible to answer questions without understanding the text. There is more to the art of asking questions than simply getting the student to parrot back a word or phrase from the text.

Look for true comprehension by:

- Asking for meaning (What is a minkle?)
- Asking for the big picture (What happened in this story?)
- Asking for inference (Why do you think Jan wanted her minkle to dreep?)
- Asking for conclusions (What can you tell about Jan's house?)
- Relating the story to real life (Do you have a minkle?)

After you have worked with your student awhile, you will be able to make valid assumptions about what your student understands and does not understand; you can then adjust the difficulty and frequency of your questions accordingly.

Questioning Techniques

What kinds of questions do the best job of building comprehension skills? One of the most common mistakes that tutors and teachers make is asking too many detailed questions (What color was the car? Who brought the potato salad?) and not enough general questions.

Detailed Questions

Detailed questions are appropriate for certain reading materials such as recipes, important news stories, or repair manuals. Detailed questions are appropriate when a character's action or the author's argument hinges on certain details. Detailed questions can also be helpful when you suspect that the student did not understand a particular sentence.

However, not every detail is important. When tutors continually ask about minor details, it suggests to the student that good readers memorize every detail as they read. You can avoid this faulty focus by asking more general questions.

General Questions

Broad, general questions help the student see the big picture. General questions don't necessarily have a right or wrong answer. General questions may invite reflection or discussion; they often activate thinking strategies such as inferring, drawing conclusions, summarizing, analyzing, or comparing.

Here are some suggestions for leading into general questions:

For any reading

- What does that mean?
- What caused this to happen?
- What were the effects of ...?
- Why ...?
- How ...?
- What is the difference between ... and ...?
- What if...?
- What do you think about the ...?

For fiction

- What happened so far in the story?
- What do you think will happen next?
- Which characters do you like? dislike?
- What was the best (worst, most interesting, funniest) ...?
- What would you have done in that situation?
- Have you ever known anyone like this person?
- Have you ever done (felt, seen, heard) anything like that?

For nonfiction

- What new information did you learn?
- How did the author organize this information?
- Do you agree or disagree? With what points? Why?
- Do you think the author was fair? honest? thorough?

Responses to Detailed or General Questions

If the student does not know the answer to a question, either ask a related question, help the student look up the answer in the passage, or just discuss or explain the answer.

Commonly Asked Questions

Should I stop my student from pointing with a finger while reading?

No. It's comprehension that counts, not the aesthetics.

What if my student reads the word correctly but mispronounces it?

It depends on the 85% rule and the student's goal (page 10). If your student is reading well (95%) or wants to get a new job (good speech makes a good impression), correct it. If your student is struggling (75%) or wants to get a driver's license (speech doesn't matter), then ignore it.

What does it mean if my student often sees a word like "large," for example, and says "big" or sees "woman" and says "lady"?

The good news is that your student has good comprehension. The guesses are appropriate for the content. If your student has had little or no phonics, try some work on consonant sounds and word families. Encourage your student to slow down.

If phonics is not or has not been helpful, it may actually be best to ignore the errors. They could be from nervousness, fatigue, or a learning disability, in which cases, time, rest, or other strategies may alleviate the problem.

Should I correct every mistake?

No. Check the three golden rules on page 10.

How to Select a Reading Strategy

The list below classifies the reading strategies (which begin on the next page) according to use.

Strategy Number and Name	Uses

— Pre-Reading —

14. Pre-Reading Survey .... fluency, comprehension
15. Hint, Hint, Hint .... difficult material and comprehension
16. Let's Find Out .... comprehension (nonfiction)
17. Tutor Rewrite .... difficult material
18. Experience Story .... fluency, change of pace, confidence

— During-Reading —

19. Echo Reading .... fluency
20. Reading Together .... fluency, pronunciation, inflection
21. Read Aloud .... fluency or difficult material
22. Questioning .... comprehension

— Post-Reading —

22. Questioning .... comprehension
23. Same and Different .... comprehension
24. Story Outline .... comprehension (fiction)
25. Mapping .... comprehension (nonfiction)

Relative Difficulty of Text

A reader at any skill level can be confronted with material that is easy or difficult for that reader. Certain tutoring strategies are more effective for easy or difficult reading material. The descriptions of the strategies on the following pages refer to the three relative levels of difficulty below.

> Independent level ----- Easy for the student
>
> Instructional level ----- Not too hard but not too easy
>
> Frustration level ------- Difficult for the student

Strategy 14

Pre-Reading Survey

Uses: Can be used with most students most of the time to improve comprehension.

Text: Instructional level (not too hard but not too easy)

Procedure:
1. With the student, examine and discuss the title, contents, subtitles, pictures, captions, excerpts, or any other material that previews the actual text.

2. If nonfiction, discuss the topic, ask questions, and fill in missing background information. Use diagrams, maps, or examples. Talk about what you might learn.

3. Preview and discuss hard words.

4. If in the middle of a book, review the story so far.

5. If there are study questions at the end of the text, consider previewing them before beginning the reading.

Hint, Hint, Hint
(Pre-Reading)

Strategy 15

Uses:
- To enable the student to read difficult material. (Students can read up to five grade levels higher using this technique.)
- To help the student focus on comprehension rather than on individual words.

Text: Frustration level (difficult for the student)

Procedure:
1. Before the lesson, study the passage and divide it into reasonable segments.

2. At the lesson, describe the content of the first segment in great detail, using many of the same words that are in the passage: "This is an article about the laws for driver's licenses. It says there are three levels of licenses for new drivers. The first level is ..." Explain difficult concepts.

3. Ask the student to read the segment that you just described.

4. Repeat Steps 2 and 3 for each succeeding segment. If the student has difficulty, use shorter segments and supply more detail.

Students can read up to five grade levels higher using this technique.

Strategy 16   Let's Find Out
(Pre-Reading)

This strategy is also known as KWL:

What do we **Know**?

What do we **Want** *to know?*

What did we **Learn**?

Uses:
- To improve comprehension.
- To provide a comprehension strategy the learner can use when reading independently.

Text: Nonfiction passage of medium difficulty (instructional level)

Procedure:
1. With the student, identify the apparent topic of the material to be read.
2. Brainstorm: What do we already know about this topic? Make a list.
3. Brainstorm: What do we want to find out about this topic? Make a second list.
4. Have the student read the passage.
5. Compare the reading with your earlier brainstorming. Was what you already knew (Step 2) confirmed? Were your questions from Step 3 answered? What more did you learn?

Tutor Rewrite
(Pre-Reading)

Strategy 17 ////////

Uses: To give the student access to difficult reading material.

Procedure: 1. Before the lesson, use the guidelines below to rewrite the difficult reading material so that it is easier to read:

- Break long sentences into two or three shorter sentences.
- Substitute short, simple words for long, difficult ones.
- Break long paragraphs into shorter ones.
- Delete less important information so that the entire selection is shorter.
- Use care to avoid changing the basic meaning of the text.

2. List difficult words at the beginning of the passage for preview.

3. If possible, type out the revised text using large, clear type and short lines.

~~The Community Center will host a series of meetings to discuss the impact of the proposed new highway construction on the community.~~

The Community Center is having some meetings.

We will talk about the new highway.

We will talk about what will happen to our community.

Strategy 18 — Experience Story

Uses:
- For students who have something to say, who like variety, who lack confidence, or who prefer a nontraditional method of learning.
- For a first-day activity, a back-up plan, or a change-of-pace plan.
- For beginning or intermediate literacy students.

Procedure:
1. Discuss a topic of interest to the student.
2. Have the student retell the experience or opinion. Write down the student's exact words—even slang and nonstandard grammar. (The student is the author; you are just the scribe.)
3. Read the story back to the student. Ask if the student wants to make any changes. Then practice reading the passage together until the student can read it alone.
4. Use words from the student's story to generate Word Study activities (see Strategy 33).

Extra options:
- Keep a copy and give one to the student.
- Keep stories in a notebook to form a journal.
- Retype stories and bind together to create a book.

Sample Experience Story
with sight words selected by the
student written on flash cards

My sister and I are very close.

sister

I talk to her on the phone

talk   phone

every weekend. She lives in

Kansas. When we were young,

young

she would sometimes take me

to the movies on Saturday. I

movies

wish she lived closer to me.

closer

Strategy 19

Echo Reading
(During-Reading)

Uses: To help the student improve fluency, phrasing, and intonation.

Text: Instructional or frustration level (medium or difficult for the student)

Procedure:
1. Read a phrase, sentence, or paragraph from the passage.
2. Ask the student to reread the same material imitating your phrasing and expression.
3. Continue alternating in the same manner.

Options:
1. By using taped readings, your student can use this technique at home. Make sure your student knows how to use the pause button.
2. Step 2 can be skipped if time is short or the student is fatigued. Just read to your student. Hearing your example will still be instructional.

Tutor: Fill out the application form

Student: Fill out the application form

Tutor: and mail it in the enclosed envelope.

Student: and mail it in the enclosed envelope.

Reading Together
(During-Reading)

Strategy 20 ///////////

Uses:
- To improve the student's reading fluency. (One study found an average gain of two grade levels for learning-disabled students using this technique for 15 minutes a day for 30 days along with other instruction.)
- To help the student get through difficult material.

Text: Frustration level (difficult for the student)

Procedure:
1. Explain to the student that you will read together.

2. Begin reading. Set the pace just a bit faster than the student would normally read. When the student hesitates, just keep going. The student will catch up at the next pause. Do not stop until you finish a paragraph or section.

{ Tutor: You may | pay your | rent in person | at the
  Student: You may | pay your | .... rent in | person at

{ Tutor: office | or you may | send a | check or
  Student: the office | or you may | send a | .... check

{ Tutor: money order to | the address below.
  Student: or money order | to the address below.

Strategy 21 — Read Aloud
(During-Reading)

Uses:
- To show students how to tackle unknown words during reading.
- To supply support during the reading process.

Text: Instructional level (not too hard but not too easy)

Procedure:
1. Ask the student to read aloud to you.

2. If the student has trouble with a word, wait a few moments to give the student a chance. Then, depending on the difficulty of the word and on the student's skills, confidence, and level of fatigue, try one of the methods below, but **do not prolong the process** to the point where the flow of the story is jeopardized:
   - Just tell the student the word, or ...
   - Say the first syllable or first sounds, or ...
   - Help the student guess the word from context, which may mean skipping the word, finishing the sentence, and coming back, or ...
   - Remind the student of a rhyming word and change the initial sound (Strategy 30), or ...
   - Cover the initial sounds or extra syllables and then uncover them (Strategy 29), or ...
   - Help the student sound out the word.

3. If the meaning may have been lost, ask the student to reread the sentence.

4. React aloud to the content and encourage your student to do the same. Express surprise, empathy, agreement, disagreement, mental images, skepticism, puzzlement, and other reactions (but do not criticize or belittle material; your student may find it interesting).

When in doubt, just tell the student the word.

Questioning
(During-Reading and Post-Reading)

Strategy 22

Uses:

- To aid comprehension for students of any level with any type of material in conjunction with any other reading strategy.

- To aid comprehension after a reading of any length (phrase, sentence, paragraph, page, story, or book).

Text: Any level

Procedure:

1. As the student reads, watch for inappropriate inflections, puzzled expressions, or other hints that the student is not comprehending. Stop and help the student find the meaning.

2. As the student reads, also stop periodically and ask, "What does that mean?" The more difficult the reading, the more frequently you should stop. If the student does not know the answer, explain or help the student find the answer.

3. Continue to monitor comprehension (see tips on pages 102-103) so that you are confident that the student is not only pronouncing the words but is understanding the message.

4. At the end of the reading, discuss the overall content and share reactions with the student.

Strategy 23 / Same and Different
(Post-Reading)

Uses: To improve analytical skills for comprehension.

Procedure:
1. Select two people, items, stories, books, or topics to be compared (can be begun before, during, or after the reading).

2. Make two overlapping circles or three columns as shown. Put one label in each circle toward the outside; in the center portion, write "both."

3. Think of ways that the two are alike and different. List the differences on the outside and the similarities in the middle.

Becky
woman
selfish
few friends
attractive

Both
single
studied hard
wanted job at hospital

Michael
man
kind
lots of friends
not attractive

Story Outline
(Post-Reading)

Strategy 24 //////////

Uses: To improve organizational skills for comprehension.

Text: Fiction, at any level of difficulty

Procedure: During or after a story, help the student identify the
setting, characters, problem or goal, events (characters'
attempts to solve the problem or achieve the goal), and
the resolution.

Setting	*Place: in a city* *Time: modern day*
Characters	*Pat* *Pat's husband* *Pat's friend* *Pat's two daughters*
Goal	*Pat must figure out how to hold her life together after her husband leaves her.*
Events	*Pat is in despair and talks to her friend.* *Pat gets a job.* *Pat goes back to school.*
Resolution	*When Pat's husband comes back, Pat decides she can do better on her own.*

Strategy 25

Mapping
(Post-Reading)

Uses:
- To improve comprehension by analysis of the topic.
- To organize information (an alternative to outlining).

Text: Nonfiction reading of any difficulty

Procedure:
1. Write the key idea in a circle in the center of the paper.

2. Help the student identify the first subtopic and write it on the map with related words as shown in the sample. (The writing on a map can be horizontal or at different angles. The sample shows a combination.)

3. Continue to build the map together. Help the student see the author's organization.

Option: This can also be done as a pre/post-reading activity by making predictions on a map before reading and revising the map later with a different color of ink.

Sample Map

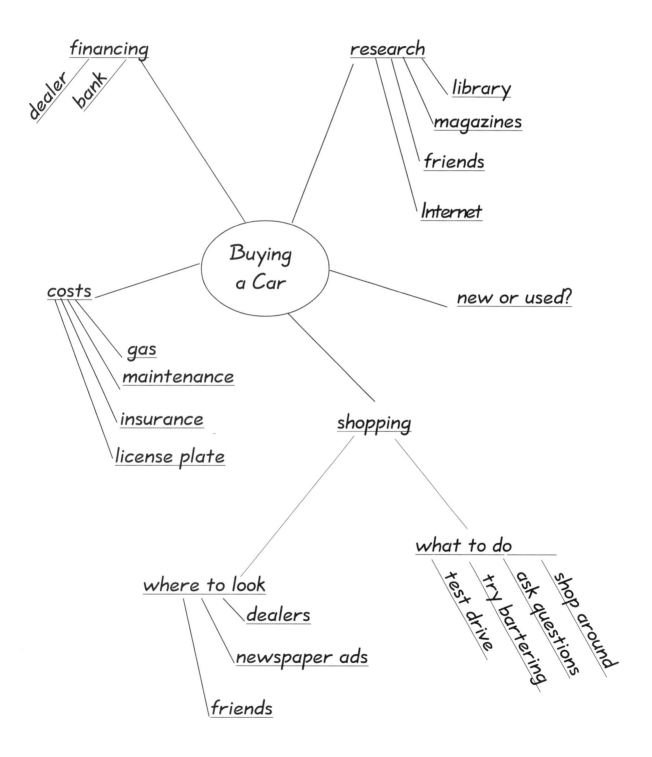

financing

dealer   bank

research

library

magazines

friends

Internet

Buying
a Car

costs

gas

maintenance

insurance

license plate

new or used?

shopping

where to look

dealers

newspaper ads

friends

what to do

test drive

try bartering

ask questions

shop around

7

Word Study

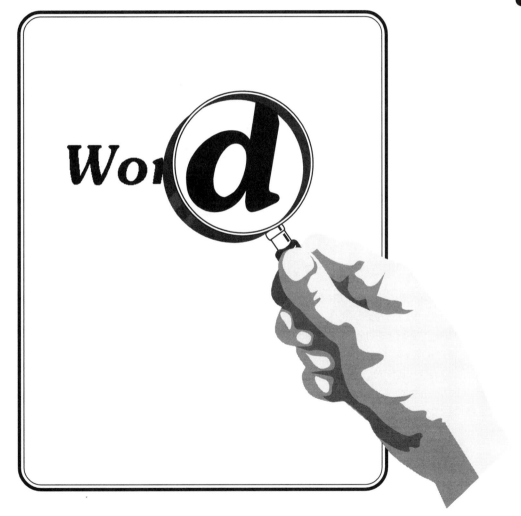

"I lost a job because I couldn't spell."

--- *Bernie, an adult literacy student*

Word Study

This chapter will provide technical background on phonics, word families, sight words, spelling, and long words, as well as 24 strategies for teaching word recognition skills.

The Word Study Part of the Lesson

The purpose of the Word Study portion of the lesson is to help the student recognize and spell individual words by becoming familiar with the patterns and the exceptions in the construction of words.

The Word Study portion of your lesson may contain one or more of these five methods for studying words:

Phonics .... learning words by combining the sounds of letters (for beginning and intermediate students)

Word Families ... learning words by recognizing rhyming patterns (for beginning and intermediate students)

Sight Words .... learning words as a complete unit (for all levels)

Long Words .... learning long words by dividing them into smaller pieces (for advanced students)

Spelling .... learning words by writing them (for all levels)

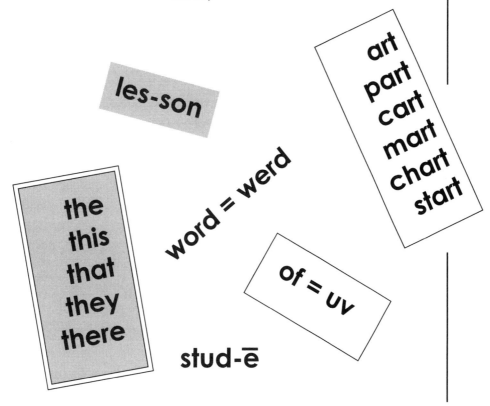

The Phonics Question

Studying vowel sounds may not be the best use of lesson time for many students.

Phonics or sight?
Debate has raged for decades over whether to teach by phonics or by sight. In fact, it is not a question of one or the other. Both methods work. It is a question of how much and for whom.

Consonants
Consonant sounds are easy to learn and fairly consistent. They provide important clues for figuring out words. Therefore, consonant sounds are valuable tools for most students.

Vowels
Vowel sounds, however, are complicated, inconsistent, and difficult to distinguish and remember. Five vowels (plus Y and W) make eighteen vowel sounds with over fifty spelling patterns, to say nothing of the exceptions. Finally, vowels often provide only frail clues for the decoding process.

Therefore, studying vowel sounds may not be the best use of lesson time for many students, if there is another way — and there is.

The solution
There is a simple tool that will allow you to take advantage of the best of phonics (the consonants) while minimizing the worst of phonics (the vowels). That tool is word families.

Word families
Word families are sets of rhyming words, such as cat, rat, hat, sat, and mat. Many adult students learn to read word families much more easily than they grasp and apply vowel sounds. Most of the strategies in this chapter build on a sequence from consonant sounds to word families to longer word patterns. This sequence works well for most students.

Alternatives
If this sequence doesn't work, try other strategies, perhaps involving more phonics, perhaps less. Your adult student can help you analyze alternatives to figure out what works and what doesn't work with your student's learning style (see Chapter 2).

Phonics Teaching Tips

The following guidelines apply to Strategies 26-30.

- Start with one or two of the easy sounds (consonant sounds for beginners; blends, digraphs, and perhaps vowels for intermediate students). Gradually introduce harder sounds (see margin).

- Limit phonics exercises to small doses with frequent review.

- Adjust the difficulty so that your student is 80 to 90% successful (the 85% Rule). To make exercises easier, limit the possible responses to fewer choices, and use easier sounds, shorter words, and easier exercises. Be prepared to shift in the middle of an exercise if needed.

- For beginning students, avoid blends: use "fee" but not "free" and "sing" but not "sting."

- Watch for patterns in your student's errors. Focus on sounds that are troublesome.

Easiest sounds:

m, b, s, d, f, t, n

- For beginners, avoid words (or overlook errors) in which the **sound** does not match the spelling, such as:

    City (begins with an S sound)
    Phone (begins with an F sound)
    Chef (begins with an SH sound)

    Cars (ends with a Z sound)
    Love (ends with a V sound)
    Laugh (ends with an F sound)

Harder sounds:

p, r, l, c, k, g, j, qu, z, v, sh

- Teach the term "vowels" as "A, E, I, O, and U," but otherwise limit your use of terminology. Your student has more urgent needs.

- If your student has great difficulty with phonics, perhaps your student is not an auditory learner. Look for other strategies.

Hardest sounds:

h, w, y, ch, th
a, e, i, o, u
blends

- Don't go backwards. If your student can already read simple words by sight or by any other method, don't spend valuable tutoring time on phonics. Build on the skills the student already uses successfully.

Beginning Students

The Word Study portion of your lesson should focus on the consonant sounds and on the short rhyming words.

If you have a beginning-level student, the Word Study portion of your lesson should focus on the consonant sounds and on the short rhyming words known as cvc (consonant-vowel-consonant) words. There are hundreds of them (like cat, rat, sat ...) and they form a good basis for recognizing words.

Pages 64-65 list suggested Word Study skills and strategies to use for beginners. If your student needs work on consonant sounds, for example, try Strategies 26 and 27. Work on only one or two skills per lesson. Review frequently.

Technical Background: Consonants

The consonants are the 21 letters that are not vowels. The next few pages contain detailed information for your reference in case questions about consonants arise. You don't have to know these details in order to tutor, and your student certainly doesn't have to know them in order to learn to read.

Most beginning students will benefit by knowing the consonant sounds. *Some* intermediate students—those who learn well by phonics and by applying rules—may benefit by knowing *some* of the more technical details. *Other* students may be overwhelmed and discouraged by such details. Proceed slowly.

The Consonant Sounds of English

Sound	Technical Details (not for most students)
B: /b/*	Usually a consistent sound as in boy, ball, and Bob. The B sounds like its own name (/b/ sounds like *"bee"*), which makes the sound easier to remember. However, the B can also be silent (comb, subtle, thumb).

* Since it is impossible to spell many sounds in isolation, two slash marks are used to indicate the sound of the letter. A good way to isolate the sound of B is to say "ab" and then remove the short A sound.

Consonant Sounds

C: /k/* A tricky letter. The sound that is taught first, /k/, or the hard C, is identical to the sound of K, (cat, car, and cut). However, the name of the letter C (*see*) sounds like an S, which causes confusion for beginners.

Intermediate students may learn that sometimes a C actually sounds like an S, also known as a soft C (city, cent, and cycle). When a C is followed by an E, I, or Y, the C will sound like an S. For example:

CE: face, cent, receive, ceiling, dance, innocence
CI: city, circle, circumstance, cider, cinch, cinema
CY: fancy, racy, bicycle, cyclone, cymbal, cyst, cynic

The C also combines with other letters to form different sounds, such as CH-, -CIAN, and -CIOUS,

D: /d/* A consistent sound as in door, dog, and dad. It sounds like its name (/d/ sounds like *dee*).

F: /f/* A consistent sound as in fun, four, and foot. The F sound can be sustained (*fff* rather than *fuh*), which makes it easier to blend with other sounds. It sounds like its name.

G: /g/* A tricky sound. Like the C, the G has a hard sound (/g/ as in go, gas, and gate) and a soft sound /j/ as in gem, gym, and gin). The soft G sound is the same as a J sound. When G is followed by an E, I, or Y, that G will usually sound like a J, or soft G. For example:

GE: age, orange, germ, fudge, general, George
GI: giraffe, gin, giant, ginger, region, religious
GY: cagy, gyrate, gym, gypsy, Egypt, apology

The soft G rule is not as reliable as the soft C rule. Some notable exceptions are get, give, and girl.

Also like the C, the name of the letter G (*jee*) sounds like the soft sound, not the hard sound. This causes beginners to think that the main sound for G is /j/, rather than /g/.

The letter U sometimes protects a hard G from a vowel that would make it soft (guess, fatigue, guide, guitar, guy).

The G is usually silent when followed by an N (gnat, sign). The GH combination can form an F sound (rough, enough), it can be silent (though, night), or it can sound like a G (ghost, spaghetti).

When C is followed by an E, I, or Y, the C will sound like an S. This rule is over 99% true!

(for your reference)

---

* Two slash marks indicate the sound of the letter. A good way to isolate the sound of the C, for example, is to say "ack" and then remove the short A sound.

Consonant Sounds

The K is silent in the combination KN.

H: /h/*	A tricky sound because it does not sound like its name and it is difficult to make (home, help, holiday). It can be silent (school, honest, John), and it often combines with other letters to make new sounds (CH, GH, PH, SH, TH, WH).
J: /j/*	A consistent sound as in jump, jam, and July (same sound as the soft G). The J sounds like its name.
K: /k/*	A consistent sound as in key, king, and kid (same sound as the hard C). It is silent in the combination KN (know, knot, knife).
L: /l/*	A consistent sound as in look, lake, and lily. The L sound can be sustained (*lll*, rather than *luh*). The L often blends with other consonants (see page 130). It can also be silent (salmon, half).
M: /m/*	A consistent and easy-to-learn sound as in mother, man, and map. It can be sustained (*mmm*, not *muh*), which helps some readers sound out words.
N: /n/*	A consistent sound as in noon, nine, and niece. It can be sustained, and it can occasionally be silent (hymn, autumn).
P: /p/*	A consistent sound as in puppy, pan, and penny. It is occasionally silent (psalm, coup, receipt). It sounds like an F when in the combination PH (phone, photo).
Q: /kw/*	Almost always paired with a U to form the sound /kw/, as in queen, quiet, and quilt. Occasionally, the U is silent and the Q sounds like a K (unique, liquor).
R: /r/*	A consistent sound as in run, race, and roar. (Although a brief "ruh" sound is more accurate, some people say "er," which is easier to use.) The R often forms blends (see page 130). When R follows a vowel, it changes the vowel sound (AR, ER, IR, OR, and UR).
S: /s/*	An easy-to-learn sound (son, snake, sale) that can be sustained (*sss*, not *suh*). It is the same sound as the soft C. The S can sound like a Z at the end of a word (rose, cars, suds). It can form blends (page 130). On rare occasion, the S is silent (corps, debris, island).
	The S makes a new sound in the combination SH. The S can sound like SH without an H present, as in sure, sugar, and -SION.

Strategies 26 and 27 can be used to teach consonant sounds.

* Two slash marks indicate the sound of the letter. One way to isolate the sound of the R, as an example, is to say "run" and then remove the "un."

Consonant Sounds

T: /t/* A fairly consistent sound, as in table, tea, and tax. It can also be silent (depot, often, castle). The T often sounds different in combinations such as TH-, -TION, and -TIOUS.

V: /v/* A consistent sound, as in valentine, vinegar, and van. It can be sustained *(vvv,* not *vuh).* It sounds like its name.

W: /w/* A difficult sound because it is inconsistent, difficult to make, and it does not sound like its name *(wuh* does not sound like doubleyoo). Sample words are woman, way, and water. The W can be silent (sword, answer, who), and it is almost always silent in the combination WR (write, wrap, wrong).

W often appears in the combination WH. Some people pronounce the sounds for W and WH differently, putting a slight puff of air at the beginning of the WH sound (more like HW). However, other people pronounce these two sounds the same. If a student pronounces the sounds for W and WH the same, they should be taught as the same sound.

W can serve as a vowel, but only in combination with A, E, or O (awning, new, owl).

X: /ks/* A tricky letter because it makes its true sound, the /ks/ sound, only at the **end** of a syllable (box, tax, exit, oxen). There is no English word that **begins** with the true sound of X. (The Xs at the beginning of xylophone and Xerox sound like Zs. The sound of the X in X-ray is *eks,* not /ks/.)

Y: /y/* A tricky sound because it is inconsistent and does not sound like its name (/y/ does not sound like *wie).* At the beginning of a word, Y is usually a consonant (yes, yellow, yonder).

At the end of a word, Y is a vowel. At the end of a one-syllable word, the Y usually sounds like a long I (my, cry, fly). At the end of a multi-syllable word, it often sounds like a long E (baby, city, daisy), but not always (rely, deny, rectify).

In the middle of a word, Y can be a consonant (backyard), but it is usually a vowel (cycle, gym, type). (See pages 203 and 217.)

Z: /z/* A consistent sound (zoo, zebra, zipper) that can be sustained *(zzz,* not *zuh).* The Z sounds like its name.

> *Some people pronounce the sounds for W and WH differently.*

> Appendix A contains words that begin with consonant sounds.

---

* Two slash marks indicate the sound of the letter. A good way to isolate the sound of the Y, for example, is to say "yell" and then remove the "ell."

Intermediate Students

If you have an intermediate-level student, the Word Study portion of your lesson should focus on words that contain blends, digraphs, and endings. This study can be based on phonics, word families, sight words, or a combination, depending on how your student learns best.

Refer to pages 66-67, for the typical Word Study skills and strategies for intermediate students. The strategies are found later in this chapter. Work on only one or two skills per lesson.

Technical Background

The information that follows should help answer questions that may arise. Additional information from pages 126-129 may also be helpful. This does not mean that you have to know this information in order to tutor or that it is necessarily desirable for your student to know it.

Blends

A blend is a string of two or three consonants (BL, STR) that blend together yet retain their original sounds.

Initial Blends

Blends with **L**	BL	CL		FL	GL	PL	SL	
Blends with **R**	BR	CR	DR	FR	GR	PR		TR
Blends with **W**			DW					TW

Blends with **S**	SC	SK	SL	SM	SN	SP	SQU	ST	SW

Triple blends	SCR	SPL	SPR	SCR					
Digraph blends	SHR	THR							

> Strategies 26 and 27 can be used to teach blend and digraph sounds.

Digraphs

A digraph is a pair of letters that forms a new sound. The original sounds of the letters are lost.

CH: A fairly consistent sound (chair, cheese, and China). (The CH is actually a T sound followed by an SH sound.) Sometimes the H is silent (echo, mechanic) and sometimes CH sounds like SH (chef, Michigan, Chicago, pistachio).

GH: A confusing pair. The GH can have 3 different sounds:

> **GH as F:** tough, rough, enough, cough, laugh
> **GH as G:** ghost, spaghetti, ghetto, aghast
> **GH silent:** dough, through, eight, caught, night

-NG: A new sound, not a blending of true N and G sounds (sing, sang, sung). Teach the -NG sound by using word families (-ing, -ang, -ung).

-NK: A blend of the NG and K sounds. The sound is really NGK. Teach this sound with word families (-ink, -ank).

PH: The same sound as F (phone, photograph, alphabet).

SH: A consistent sound that can be sustained (ship, she, shade).

TH: There are actually two TH sounds:
> Whispered (thank, three, thumb, Thursday)
> Buzzy (the, this, these, they, there)

(Other sample words are on page 207.)

Say the sounds slowly to hear the difference, or put your fingertips on your throat to feel the difference.

Dictionaries distinguish between the two TH sounds with slightly different symbols. Most students do not need to know that two TH sounds exist.

WH: If your student pronounces WH the same as W, teach your student that WH makes the same sound as W. (Test with whether/weather and which/witch). But if your student pronounces the WH like an HW, putting a subtle puff of air before the W, teach the W and WH as separate sounds.

Digraphs form a new sound; blends keep their original sounds.

> Appendix B contains words that begin with these blends and digraphs.

Short A

Each vowel has two main sounds, a short sound and a long sound.

Long A

Vowel Sounds

There are five vowels: A, E, I, O, U (and sometimes Y and W). The five main vowels (A, E, I, O, U) have two main sounds, a short sound and a long sound, as well as several other sounds.

Every word has at least one vowel.

Every syllable has one — and only one — vowel sound (although two or three vowels may be used to make that one sound). Notice the distinction between vowels and vowel sounds. Although there are five vowels (letters), there are eighteen vowel sounds, as shown on the next page.

These eighteen vowel sounds have over fifty spellings. For example, the long E sound can be spelled with one E (me), with two Es (see), with an EA (seam), with an EY (key), or with an EI (ceiling). Appendix D shows some of these complex patterns. However, there is no need — and in fact, it is usually counter-productive — for a student to try to learn all of these vowel patterns. The basic patterns on the next page are usually sufficient.

How to Teach Vowel Sounds

First, decide *if* you should teach vowel sounds. Many students learn better using just word families (see page 124 and Strategies 30-32).

If your student responds well to phonics, you can teach vowel sounds by using Strategies 26 and 27 to introduce and practice the sounds (see also Appendix C) and by using Strategy 28 to explain and practice some of the vowel rules such as those on the next page.

Regional Differences

If you think your student has an accent, just remember that your student thinks *you* have an accent. You probably pronounce certain vowel sounds differently. Do not try to change your student's "accent" (unless that is your student's wish). Just say, "For you, the short O sound is this, and for me the short O sound is that. They are both right; they are just different because we come from different parts of the country."

The Eighteen Vowel Sounds of English

5 Short Vowel Sounds

ă	apple
ĕ	echo
ĭ	igloo
ŏ	October
ŭ	umbrella

If a word has only one vowel, it is usually short.

    cat   red   list   hot   pup

A phrase that contains all five sounds may help:

    Fat Ed is not up.   **Ann sells pink hot tubs.**
    An egg is on us.   **Fat men in a hot tub...**

*Reminder:
This is
for your
reference, not
necessarily for
the student to
learn.*

5 Long Vowel Sounds

A long vowel says its own name.

ā	ate
ē	eat
ī	ice
ō	oats
ū	use

1. An E at the end of a word makes the vowel long.

    can ... cāne   not..... nōte   kit ... kīte

(Rule 1 is unreliable for multi-syllable words.)

2. When two vowels go walking, the first one does the talking. (The first is long; the second is silent.)

    seat   coat   maid   toad

(Rule 2 applies most often to only four pairs of vowels: AI, EA, EE, and OA.)

Strategies 26 and 27 can be used to teach vowel sounds.

5 Other Vowel Sounds

aw/au	saw/sauce
oy/oi	boy/boil
ow/ou	cow/count
o͞o	loose tooth
o͝o	good book

Usually the W and Y (AW, OY, and OW) are used at the end of a word, and the other pairs (AU, OI, and OU) are used in the middle.

The easiest way to distinguish the two sounds for OO is to recognize the patterns on page 242.

Appendix C lists words that contain these vowel sounds.

3 R-Controlled Sounds

An R changes the sound of the vowel.

ar	art
er/ir/ur	urgent
or	order

ER, IR, and UR have the same sound.

Appendix D shows the spellings of these sounds.

134

gĭvé*

cōást

knīfé

Tutor Check 1 — Basic Phonics

If you can recognize silent letters and long and short vowels, then you can teach basic phonics to your student. It can often be helpful, when the student doesn't know a word, to say, "That E is silent," or "That's a long O." Check your basic phonics skills on this page. (If you are not a phonetic learner yourself, just use other strategies or request a more advanced student.)

> 1. Say the word slowly. Cross off any silent consonants.
>
> 2. Mark every vowel as long (ā), short (ă), or silent (ǿ).

1. boat	fine	wrap	beet
2. ghost	light	knit	grief
3. cute	have	save	know
4. wrote	steam	depot	guide
5. bread	sign	Spain	great

Answers

1. bōát	fīné	wráp	bēét
2. ghōst	līght	knĭt	grēf*
3. cūté	hăvé*	sāvé	knōw
4. wrōté	stēám	dēpōt	gúidé
5. brĕád*	sīgn	Spáin	grĕát*

*These words are exceptions to the long-vowel rules on page 133.

Tutor Check 2 — Tricky Phonics

The words on this page contain one or more letters that tend to mislead new readers. See if you can identify the deceptive letters and their sounds. While it is not necessary for either you or your student to be this skilled in phonics, a phonetically inclined student may appreciate tips such as, "This is a soft C," or "This O-R sounds like an E-R."

> 1. Mark consonants and vowels as on the preceding page.
>
> 2. Underline any pair of letters that combine to make a new sound (see pages 127, 131, and 133).
>
> 3. If any letter or group of letters makes a sound other than its usual sound, write the new sound above the letter or letters. TIP: Say the word in slow motion and listen for each sound.

1. rose	cage	wonder	gypsy
2. lacy	actor	agent	accent
3. used	ready	warn	receipt
4. easy	radio	action	region
5. chef	niece	moth	edge

shŏve*

spāce (s)

shun
nātion

Answers

1. rōse (z)	cāge (J)	wŏnder (u)	gypsy (Ji ē)
2. lācy (s ē)	actor (er)	āgent (J)	accent (K S)
3. ūsed (z)	rĕady (ē)	warn (or)	recēipt (s)
4. ēasy (z ē)	rādīo (ē)	action (shun)	region (Jun)
5. chef (sh)	nīece (s)	moth (au)	edge (J) or edge (J)

Add ES to words ending in S, X, Z, CH, or SH.

Strategy 38 explains how to teach spelling patterns for endings.

Spelling Rules for Adding -S

Note: Introduce and practice only one rule at a time.

Category	Rule
Most words	Just add S to **most** words. For example: girls, cars, stores, books, dogs
-S, -X, -Z, -CH, and -SH	Add ES to words ending in S, X, Z, CH, or SH. (You can hear the extra syllable when you say the word.) For example: S: dresses, glasses, bosses, buses X: boxes, foxes, taxes, fixes Z: buzzes, fizzes, blitzes CH: watches, catches, inches, lunches SH: wishes, dishes, ashes, pushes
-Y	For words ending in a consonant and a Y, change the Y to I and add ES. For example: flies, cries, dries, tries, skies babies, ladies, marries, cities (If the word ends in a vowel and a Y, just add S: boys, days, keys, monkeys.)
-F and -FE	For many words that end in F and FE, change the F or FE to VES. loaves, leaves, wolves, shelves wives, lives, knives, thieves Exceptions: cliffs, cuffs, roofs, etc.

Spelling Rules for Adding -ER, -ED, -EST, and -ING

Category	Rule
-E	For words ending in E, drop the E and add the ending. For example: … ER baker, racer, maker, nicer, later … ED baked, loved, faded, hoped, lived … EST latest, nicest, tamest, ripest, widest … ING baking, loving, fading, hoping, living
-Y	For words ending in a consonant and a Y, change the Y to I and add the ending—*except* for the ending -ING. For example: … IER happier, funnier, lazier, crazier … IED tried, dried, married, carried, hurried … IEST happiest, funniest, laziest, craziest … YING trying, flying, marrying, hurrying
One vowel and one consonant	For *one*-syllable words ending in *one* vowel and *one* consonant, double the final consonant and add the ending (the 1-1-1 rule). For example: stop — stopped, stopping big — bigger, biggest hug — hugger, hugged, hugging slip — slipper, slipped, slipping Exceptions: bus — busing and words ending in X: tax — taxed In contrast, if the word ends in **two** vowels and one consonant or one vowel and **two** consonants, do not double the consonant: looked, looking, waiter, waited, waiting faster, fastest, camper, camped, camping

Introduce and practice only one rule at a time.

Advanced Students

If you have an advanced-level student, the Word Study portion of your lesson should focus on reading and spelling words of two or more syllables. Refer to pages 68-69 for typical word study goals and strategies for advanced students.

Advanced Student Needs

Advanced students can usually read most of the short, everyday words and are now hampered only by long, new words—the final hurdle.

Many students find long words intimidating and frustrating. Such students will benefit from (1) understanding that long words are made of short parts that usually fit known word family patterns and (2) knowing where to cut the word, **even before knowing what the word is**, in order to figure out each part.

Solutions

Strategies 44-49 provide a teaching sequence to help your advanced-level student acquire these skills. You will be introduced to three rules for dividing words into pieces.

It is important that the student be comfortable with word family patterns—including nonsense words—before beginning this series (Strategies 30-32). Figuring out the word "lumber" depends on recognizing that "lum" is just like "gum" and "ber" is just like "her."

The most difficult aspect of teaching the three rules is to understand the student's perspective. Tutors tend to see the three rules as a technique for dividing words into syllables. They are not that at all.

Traditional syllable rules are for readers who already know what the word is. LITSTART's three long-word rules are for students who do **not** know what the word is and are trying to figure it out. The traditional syllable rules are used on known words; LITSTART's three long-word rules are used on unknown words.

Traditional syllable rules are used on known words; LITSTART's rules are used on __unknown__ words.

How to Select a Word Study Strategy

The chart below differentiates the Word Study strategies (which begin on the next page) on the basis of the level of the student (1= ESL Level 1, 2 = ESL Level 2, B= Beginning, I = Intermediate, A = Advanced). See also pages 60-69.

Strategy 26

Personal Phonics Cards

Uses: To study letters and sounds by using key words

Procedure:

1. With the student, generate a list of words that begin with a particular sound. Write the words on scrap paper and help the student read the list and isolate the sound.

2. Let your student select a key word from the list. Help your student transfer the key word and other chosen words to the card. For study at home, put a sketch or picture of the key word on the back of the card.

3. After making several cards, ask the student to select a card and:
   - Say the key word (basketball).
   - Say the sound (/b/).
   - Say the letter (B).

4. If all three responses are correct, set the card aside. If any response is not correct, put the card at the bottom of the stack to try again. Continue until all cards are set aside. Shuffle the cards before starting again.

5. Review regularly. Retire cards that are consistently correct.

Appendix A contains words that begin with single consonants.

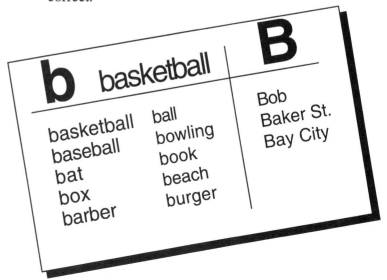

b basketball	B
basketball ball baseball bowling bat book box beach barber burger	Bob Baker St. Bay City

What Do You Hear?

Strategy 27 //////////

Uses:

To help students learn the sounds of consonants, vowels, blends, or digraphs.

Procedure:

Try **one** of the oral exercises below with word lists you have prepared in advance. (See Appendices A, B, and C and the tips on page 125.)

Exercises:

Listed generally **in order of difficulty**:

A. I will say a word. If you hear the sound /m/* (write M) on the beginning of the word, say "M" or "yes." If you do not hear /m/, say "no." (After success, change letters.)

B. I will say a word that begins with either an /m/ sound or a /b/ sound (write M and B). You say the letter. (After success, add letters or change letters.)

C. I will say a word. You say the sound (and the letter) you hear at the beginning of the word. (Use a few or many letters based on the student's need.)

D. I will say a letter. You say the sound (or the key word and the sound).

E. I will say a sound. You say the letter. (Show the possible answers, just a few at first.)

F. I will say a word. You say the sound at the end (or beginning and end) of the word.

Easiest sounds:

m, b, s, d, f, t, n

Harder sounds:

p, r, l, c, k, g, j, qu, z, v, sh

Hardest sounds:

h, w, y, ch, th, a, e, i, o, u, blends

Appendix B contains words that begin with blends and digraphs.

Appendix C contains words that begin with vowels.

* Two slash marks indicate the sound of the letter.

Strategy 28 — Sound It Out

rīdé
lāké
rōpé
nāmé
cūté

tube
file
safe
bone
vase

Uses: To teach rules of phonics to students who like rules and who can sound out some words.

Procedure: Note: Try Strategies 30-32 first. Many students get more benefit with less effort by using word families.

1. Before the lesson, create or find a list of words that contain some sounds or a pattern that you think it might be helpful for the student to understand. (Check tips on page 125.)

2. Introduce the sound or rule by using 3 or 4 words (preferably from the student's reading) that contain the pattern. Either explain the pattern or help the student discover the pattern by asking questions.

   Note: If possible, when sounding out a word, sustain the sound of one letter without a break before saying the next sound. Say "mmmaaannn" rather than "mmm---aaa---nnn." (However, many consonant sounds can't be sustained.)

3. Help the student practice applying the rule using the list of words prepared in Step 1.

4. Transfer the practice of sounding out words to reading in context, taking care not to prolong phonics attempts to the point where the flow of a story is disrupted. (When in doubt, just tell the student the word.)

Tip: A student who knows all the sounds but has persistent difficulty blending them together may not be a good phonics candidate. Try Strategies 30-32 or 33 or just focus on reading and spelling. Some students learn words best in context.

Cover It Up

Strategy 29

Uses: To provide an alternative method for sounding out words (can be used during reading).

Procedure:
1. With a card or a finger, cover the initial consonant(s) and expose the vowel and the end of the word or syllable (a word family pattern).

2. Ask the student to read the exposed part, or help the student think of one or more words with the same letters (rhyming words), whichever method works best for your student.

3. Uncover one consonant and ask the student to read the new "word." If there are other consonants, add them one at a time from right to left.

4. (If a list of words is being practiced, review the list, repeating Steps 1-3 when necessary.)

NOTE: For more advanced students, cover prefixes, suffixes, or extra syllables.

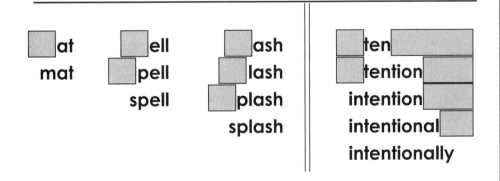

Strategy 30 — Word Family Patterns

Uses:

- To help students figure out words through rhyming patterns.

- To provide students who have difficulty with vowel sounds with an alternative method for figuring out words.

ap
map
rap
sap
tap
nap
gap
cap
zap

et
get
bet
wet
net
pet
set
let
vet
met
jet
yet

Procedure:

1. Select a word family pattern (for example, -ap, -ell, -ite) from your student's reading material or from Appendix E or F. (Alternatively, create a card for each pattern.)

2. Ask your student to read the heading. If your student hesitates, say "a-p says ap."

3. Point to or write a rhyming word underneath. Ask the student for the word. If the student doesn't know the word, supply it.

4. Continue adding and reading rhyming words.

5. Ask the student to reread the list once or twice.

6. For extra review, point to the words in random order on the list.

7. Practice only two or three rhyming patterns at each lesson, but practice a little during every lesson.

Appendices E and F contain word family listings.

How Many Meanings?

Strategy 31 //////////

Uses:
- To illustrate multiple meanings of words.
- To help clarify subtle sound differences between such words as *pan* and *pen*, or *ban* and *band*.

Procedure:
1. Preview a word family list using Strategy 30.

2. Ask the student what the first word means. Accept any reasonable description. (A "definition" for *can* might be "like a can of beans.") Together, try to think of additional meanings.

3. Continue together down the list, generating as many meanings as you can for each word. Many three-letter words have multiple meanings, a gold mine of teaching opportunities. For example:

    run   ... **run** down the street
                ... a **run** in her stockings
                ... **run** for president
                ... **run** the copy machine
                ... a home **run**
                ... **run** out of coffee

4. Clarify meanings as needed. When your student gives an incorrect definition (such as "a rubber band" for *ban),* show the student both words and explain the difference.

Many three-letter words have multiple meanings, a gold mine of teaching opportunities.

Strategy 32 — Nonsense Words

id
bid
did
fid
hid
jid
kid
lid
mid
nid
pid
quid
rid
sid
tid
vid
wid
yid
zid

Uses:
- To provide more practice in family patterns.
- To prepare the student to read longer words.

Procedure:
1. Follow Strategy 30 but use all the consonants.
2. Explain to your student that some of the words are not real words but may be parts of longer words. For example:

> **mem** is part of member, remember, memory, memorial, memo, Memphis, ...

> **tem** is part of temper, temperature, temple, stem, item, September, temporary, ...

Tips:
- To avoid dealing with soft Cs and Gs, skip Cs and Gs when practicing patterns that begin with E or I.
- An easy way to generate these words is to make flash cards for family patterns and smaller cards for consonants as shown. Pile the consonants on top of a family card and flip through the consonants.
- If off-color words would offend you or your student, remove potentially troublesome consonants beforehand.

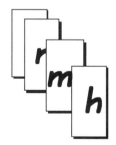

Applied Sight Words

Strategy 33 //////////

Uses:
- To provide practice, especially for visual or kinesthetic learners, on words that are not phonetic or that cause difficulty.

- For ESL students who need to learn critical words by sight before developing reading skills.

Procedure:
1. Ask the student to select a few words to study from a passage, an Experience Story (Strategy 18), or ESL Picture Cards.

2. Help the student print the words on cards. (If the student will study the cards at home, put a phrase, sketch, or clue on the back for checking purposes.)

3. Use the cards in one or more of these activities:

   A. FLASH CARDS: Mix the cards, stack them, and help the student read them as flash cards. Let the student decide after each card whether to set that card aside or to put it at the bottom of the stack to try again.

   B. MATCH: Help the student match word cards to words in a story (see page 111).

   C. SEARCH: Ask the student to choose a card, look for that word in a newspaper, and circle it each time it is found.

   D. PUZZLES: Spread a few cards on the table. Give a clue such as "Blank time is it?" Ask the student to find the missing word card to complete the sentence.

The best way to teach most sight words is just to tell the student the word during reading.

Appendix K contains sight words.

Appendices L and M contain signs that some students may want to learn by sight.

What is your name?

Strategy 34 — Workbooks

Uses:

- To provide a variety of activities from which to choose for work during the lesson and at home.

- To save preparation time.

- To create a concrete measure of progress, which can motivate certain students.

    Warning: Conversely, workbooks may evoke negative associations among other students.

Procedure:

1. With your student, select an adult workbook that looks enjoyable and educational.

2. If possible, arrange for your student to write in the book. This is more satisfying for the student, it respects copyright law, and it usually costs less than photocopying.

3. If you find a type of exercise that seems beneficial to your student, consider creating similar exercises on your own.

4. Don't waste your student's time with exercises that are too easy, too difficult, too time-consuming, irrelevant, or otherwise inappropriate for your student. Trust your instincts. Skip those pages.

Puzzles and Games

Strategy 35

Uses:
- As a back-up plan or for variation from a routine.
- As a special activity to celebrate accomplishments or holidays.

Procedure:
1. Examine potential puzzles and games to determine if the difficulty level is appropriate for your student. Consider computer word games, Scrabble, Scrabble for Juniors, Boggle, Wheel of Fortune, other board games, easy crossword puzzles, word searches, hangman, and other paper/pencil games.

2. Try the games with your student. Be flexible about modifying the rules and giving hints. Try playing games as partners rather than as competitors.

Beware: Avoid the trap of using puzzles and games routinely. Although they are fun and easy for the tutor, most games and puzzles do not produce as much learning for the amount of time consumed as do other activities.

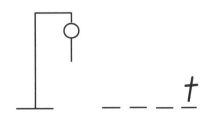

Strategy 36 Spelling Prep

Uses:
- To help the auditory student learn consonant or vowel sounds.
- To develop initial spelling skills.

Procedure:
1. Try **one** of the exercises below with word lists you have prepared in advance.
2. Over the course of many lessons, add sounds and progress to more difficult exercises using the 85% rule (page 10) to guide your pacing.
3. See tips on page 125.

Exercises:
Listed in **order of difficulty**:

A. I will say a word that begins with either the sound /m/* (write "m") or the sound /b/* (write "b"). You write the letter that you hear at the beginning of the word.

(After the student masters this skill, change letters. Later, offer 3, 4, or 5 choices.)

B. I will say a word (don't offer possible answers this time). You write the letter you hear at the beginning of the word.

C. I will say a word. You write the letter that you hear at the end of the word.

D. I will say a word. You write the letter that you hear at the beginning and the end of the word.

* Two slash marks indicate the sound of the letter.

Spelling Patterns 1 / *Strategy 37*

Uses:
- To reinforce word patterns taught during the reading part of the lesson.
- To allow the student to spell new words without studying beforehand.

Procedure:
1. Select two or three word family patterns from Appendices E or F.
2. Say the first word clearly, exaggerating the sounds to show the student how to listen for sounds.
3. Use the word in a sentence.
4. Repeat the word as the student writes the word.
5. If the word is right, say so. If the word is wrong, help the student fix the word.
6. Repeat Steps 2-5 with additional words.

at	end	ight
bat	send	light
cat	lend	sight
hat	bend	slight
mat	mend	flight
pat	blend	right
sat	spend	bright

> Appendices E and F contain word family lists.

Strategy 38 Spelling Patterns 2

Uses: To expand the spelling ability of intermediate and advanced students by building on patterns.

Procedure: 1. After the student is competent at spelling basic word family patterns (Strategy 37), begin to mix in plural forms of the words using the same format as in Strategy 37 for giving and checking the words.

2. As the student gains mastery, gradually introduce the endings -ED, -ING, -ER, -EST, and -LY, maintaining the format of Strategy 37. Explain new spelling rules (pages 136-137) as needed. Adjust the difficulty according to the 85% rule (page 10).

3. For advanced students, introduce words of two and three syllables such as those in Appendix H. Help the student by pronouncing the syllables separately and distinctly.

ap	**ap**	
map	napped	trapped
maps	slapped	trapping
caps	tapped	trapper
flap	tapping	snapper
snaps	clapped	napping
trap	clapping	flapping
Step 1	Step 2	

Copy Cat

Uses:
- To help the student learn to spell non-phonetic words (as in Appendix K).
- For students who have low reading skills but urgent spelling needs.
- For students who learn well by rote drilling in visual, auditory, and kinesthetic modes or who do not respond well to analytic strategies.
- For the student to study at home.

Procedure:
1. Write the word the student wants to learn in large letters with a marker to make a dark thick line. (This could also be done on a chalkboard.)
2. Invite the student to say the word and trace your word once or several times with a pen or pencil, saying the letters aloud as they are traced.
3. Ask the student to copy the word under your word once or several times, saying the letters aloud.
4. Have the student cover all copies of the word, write it from memory once or several times, and check it.

Note: It is the student who should decide how many repetitions of each step are needed.

Appendix K contains words that are not phonetic.

//////// **Strategy 40** **Close Your Eyes**

Uses: For visual learners to practice spelling.

Procedure: 1. Print the student's name and show it to the student. (The name is used to illustrate the technique.)

2. Say, "Now close your eyes and picture a blackboard in your mind. Can you see it? Now look at the upper left part of that blackboard and try to see your name written there. Can you see it?" If the student has trouble, discontinue this strategy.

3. If the student can visualize the name, repeat Steps 1 and 2 with a new word. Again, if the student has trouble, discontinue the strategy.

4. Ask the student, with eyes closed, to "copy" the new word on the table with a finger one or more times while "looking" at the word on the "blackboard."

5. Have the student, with eyes open, write the word on a piece of paper.

6. Make corrections or repeat as needed.

Options: • Experimenting with colors in the mind may help: perhaps a green word on a white board or a white word on a blue board would work better.

• Some students may wish to spell the word aloud as they work; others may not.

Look, Ma, No Pen! *Strategy 41*

Uses:

- For variety.

- For kinesthetic or tactile learners.

- For students who have difficulty with penmanship or who have certain physical impairments.

Procedure: Use any of the other Word Study strategies (26-49) or Writing strategies (50-60), but suggest that the student, instead of writing the word on paper, use one of these other modes:

- Use chalk on a blackboard or a marker on a whiteboard. (The larger motion helps some students.)

- Use a large marker on the back of scrap paper (one word per page).

- Move Scrabble tiles, lettered dice, magnetic letters, wooden letters, flash cards, or letters cut out of sandpaper or textured material. (The 3-D and textured letters help tactile students who profit from "feeling" the letters.)

- Type the words on a typewriter or computer keyboard.

- Write the words in a tray of sand or salt.

- Spell the words aloud without writing them at all.

Strategy 42 — Spelling Tricks

Uses: To help students learn non-phonetic spelling words (as in Appendix K).

Procedure:
1. Together with the student, examine each word to be learned and identify some clue or device to remember the word without having to resort to rote drill (see next page for samples).

2. After a trick is selected, have the student try writing the word.

3. Review after 3 or 4 new words and again periodically.

Appendix K contains lists of non-phonetic words.

Spelling Tricks for Non-phonetic Words

Different memory tricks work for different people and for different words. What works for you may not work for your student. Be creative and invent your own tricks.

Tricky Letters: Analyze each syllable and isolate the tricky letters. Then memorize only the tricky part.

> *For example:*
>
> The word *debt* makes sense except for the B.
> *Beau-ti-ful* makes sense except for the EAU.

Mispronunciation: Mispronounce the word according to its spelling.

> *For example:*
>
> Pronounce *some* to rhyme with *home*.
> Pronounce the B in *comb* and *thumb*.
> Pronounce *Wednesday* as three syllables: Wed-ness-day.
> Pronounce *chef* not as *shef*, but with a true CH as in *chief*.

Little words: Look for little words in bigger words.

> *For example:*
>
> There's a *gain* in *again*.
> There's an *eat* in *great*.
> There's a *ran* in *orange*.

Association: Associate the difficult part of the spelling with another word that shares part of the spelling pattern.

> *For example:*
>
> The princi*pal* is your *pal*.
> A princip*le* is a ru*le*. (Both end in -LE.)
> Station*ery* is made of pap*er*; you use it to write a lett*er*.
> You h*ear* with your *ear*.
> H*ere*, th*ere*, and wh*ere* are all places.
> There, their, and they're all start with *the*.

Strategy 43

Recorded Spelling

Uses: For practice at home.

Procedures: — *A. For auditory learners to study words* —

1. Record (or help the student record) a list of words to study. Say each word clearly, then spell it slowly, then say it again: "was, W-A-S, was."

2. Encourage the student to listen to the tape at home.

— *B. To practice words* —

1. Use a hand-held spelling computer that "pronounces" words or record your own list before the lesson using the following format:

   a. Say the word clearly and slowly.

   b. Use the word in a sentence.

   c. Say the word again.

   d. Pause long enough for the student to write the word.

   e. Say the word again and spell it slowly so the student can check the word immediately.

2. Make sure the student knows how to use the tape player or computer. Encourage the student to repeat the exercise until the words are mastered.

3. At the following lesson, check your student on the words.

   (If you use this strategy regularly, you might try having the student use the "pause" button instead of building in a pause.)

Long Words A:
Compound Words *Strategy 44* ////////

Uses:
- To help intermediate and advanced students see long words as a string of short words.

- To prepare the student for the concept of cutting long, unknown, non-compound words.

Procedure:
1. Starting with a sample from the student's reading, demonstrate that some long words are just combinations of short words. (Use a different colored ink to draw the line.)

   foot|print   hand|shake   ear|ring

2. Discuss how each word probably evolved from the combination of the meanings of the smaller words.

3. Using 10 or 20 words from Appendix G, help the student divide, read, and define the words.

4. Review and add more words at each lesson. (Exercises like this are most effective when practiced for short periods of time and spread over several lessons.)

COMPOUND WORDS

A compound word is a longer word composed of two shorter words.

Appendix G contains compound words.

Strategy 45

Long Words B: The Two-Consonant Rule

Traditional syllable rules are used on known words; LITSTART's three rules are used on <u>unknown</u> words.

Uses: To help advanced students figure out long words.

Procedure: 1. Demonstrate the three steps below for cutting an unknown long word into small pieces.

    A. Find the vowels and mark them with a dot.

      garden   attack   trumpet

    B. Look between the vowels. How many consonants are there? (two)

      garden   attack   trumpet
      • 1 - 2 •   • 1 - 2 •   • 1 - 2 •

    C. If there are two consonants, cut the word between the two consonants. Read the word.

      gar/den   at/tack   trum/pet

2. Using a list of 20-30 words (see Appendix H1), assist the student in marking vowels, dividing words, reading words, and defining words. Review the list.

3. At each lesson, review the previous list and add 20-30 more words. Continue for several lessons.

4. IMPORTANT: Do not proceed to the next rule until the student is proficient with this one.

Appendix H1 contains words that follow the Two-Consonant Rule.

The Two-Consonant Rule

If there are two consonants between the vowels, cut the word between the consonants.

    in/to   les/son   traf/fic   fen/der

Tutor Check 3 — Long Words with Two Consonants

It is difficult to understand the student's perspective in the previous strategy. Remember, the student does not know the word. Instead of seeing words, suppose you saw just a string of consonants (Cs) and vowels (Vs). Instead of "trespass," suppose you saw "ccvccvcc." Could you divide the word into syllables? If you use the two-consonant rule, you can.

Notice that not all pairs of consonants are divided, only those between two vowels. That is the purpose of marking the vowels first.

Try dividing the words below using the steps on the preceding page. Then check your answers at the bottom of this page.

1. v c c v c	4. c v c c v c c v c
2. c c v c c v c	5. c v c c v c c
3. c v c c v c	6. c c v c c v c

Warning: This page is not for students!

If you got those right, look over Strategy 46 on the next page and then try the harder words below. Es and Ys are real Es and Ys.

7. v c c v c c v c e	10. c v c c v v c c
8. c v c c v c c y	11. c c v c c y
9. c v c c v v c	12. c c c v c c v c

Answers

1. vc/cvc (attic)	4. cvc/cvc/cvc (carpenter)
2. ccvc/cvc (problem)	5. cvc/cvccc (midnight)
3. cvc/cvc (public)	6. ccvc/cvc (thunder)

----

7. vc/cvc/cvce (advertise)	10. cvc/cvvcc (discount)
8. cvc/cvc/cy (suddenly)	11. ccvc/cy (twenty)
9. cvc/cvvc (cartoon)	12. cccvc/cvc (splendid)

162

Strategy 46

Long Words C: Two-Consonant Specials

If there are two consonants between the vowels, cut the word between the consonants.

Uses: To expand the usefulness of the Two-Consonant Rule (page 160).

Procedure: 1. Demonstrate special cases for cutting words.

- If the word ends with an E, cross it off and ignore it.

    ad/vancé   pol/luté   con/vincé

- If the word ends with a Y, count the Y as a vowel.

    hap/py   dir/ty   grum/py

- Count two vowels together as one.

    car/toon   ac/tion*   main/tain

- If the word has three or more vowels, continue dividing using the same procedure.

    Sep/tem/ber sil/ver/waré in/ter/feré

2. Using a list of appropriate words (see Appendix H2), guide the student in dividing, reading, and defining words.

3. Review and add more words each lesson.

Appendix H2 contains words that are special cases of the Two-Consonant Rule.

* Teach nonphonetic syllables such as "-tion" as a unit: "shun."

Long Words D:

The One-Consonant Rule

Strategy 47 ////////

Uses: To expand skills in figuring out long words.

Procedure:
1. Review the Two-Consonant Rule and explain that there is a different rule when there is only one consonant between the vowels. Demonstrate:

    A. Find the vowels and mark them with a dot.

    t i g e r   h u m i d   m o m e n t
    · ·   · ·   · ·

    B. Count the letters between the marked vowels (in these cases, only one).

    t i g e r   h u m i d   m o m e n t
    · 1 ·   · 1 ·   · 1 ·

    C. Cut the word before the consonant and make the first vowel long (it says its own name).

    t ī|g e r   h ū|m i d   m ō|m e n t
    ·   ·   ·

2. Using a list of 20 to 30 words (see Appendix H3), assist the student in marking vowels, dividing words, reading words, and defining words.

3. Review and add 20 to 30 more words each lesson.

The One-Consonant Rule

If there is only one consonant between the vowels, divide the word before the consonant and make the first vowel long.

ē|v e n   s ō|b e r   p r ē|t e n d   s h ā|k y
· ·   · ·   · ·   · ·

Appendix H3 contains words that follow the One-Consonant Rule.

Strategy 48

Long Words E: Combinations

Uses: To provide practice using two long-word rules together.

Procedure:

1. After the student has mastered the Two-Consonant Rule and the One-Consonant Rule, demonstrate how to use the two rules together:

   A. Mark the vowels with a dot.

   agency   beginning   computer

   B. How many consonants are between the vowels? (sometimes two, sometimes one)

   agency   beginning   computer
   1   1-2   1   1-2   1-2   1

   C. Cut the word according to the two rules.

   ā/gen/cy   bē/gin/ning   com/pū/ter

   D. (If you wish, mark and discuss additional phonics clues like silent letters and soft Cs and Gs.)

   ā/gen/cy   bē/gin/ning   com/pū/ter

2. Practice with words such as those in Appendix H4.

Appendix H4 contains words that follow combinations of the Two-Consonant Rule and the One-Consonant Rule.

Tutor Check 4 — Long Words Mixed

The rules covered in the preceding five strategies are designed not to help students divide words into syllables, but to help students figure out long words.

It may be difficult to appreciate the impact of these strategies because you know what the words are and probably tend to divide the words based on the sound of the words. Students, who theoretically do not know the words, cannot do this.

The exercise below illustrates how students use the rules. The words below are real, but all vowels have been changed to Vs and all consonants have been changed to Cs. The letter E represents itself.

Try to divide the words below using the Two-Consonant and One-Consonant rules.

1. cvcvc   4. vcvc

2. ccvcvc   5. cvcvvc

3. ccvcvcc   6. cvcvce

- -

7. cvcvccvc   10. vccvccvcvvc

8. cvccvcv   11. cvcvccvc

9. vcvvccvcc   12. ccvcvccvvc

Answers

1. cv̄/cvc (paper)   4. v̄/cvc (omit)
2. ccv̄/cvc (spoken)   5. cv̄/cvvc (retail)
3. ccv̄/cvcc (pretend)   6. cv̄/cvce̸ (polite)
- -
7. cv̄/cvc/cvc (November)   10. vc/cvc/cv̄/cvvc (information)
8. cvc/cv̄/cv (tornado)   11. cv̄/cvc/cvc (cucumber)
9. v̄/cvvc/cvcc (equipment) 12. ccv̄/cvc/cvvc (cloverleaf)

Strategy 49

Long Words F: The One-Consonant— Oops Rule

Uses: To complete the student's tool kit with the third and last rule for figuring out long words.

Procedure: 1. After the student has **mastered** the Two-Consonant and One-Consonant Rules, demonstrate the last rule:

A. Mark the vowels.

lemon   habit   credit

B. Count the letters between the vowels. (one)

lemon   habit   credit
· 1 ·   · 1 ·   · 1 ·

C. Apply the One-Consonant Rule (page 163).

lē/mon   hā/bit   crē/dit

D. Oops! Sometimes the One-Consonant Rule doesn't work! If you don't recognize the word, divide the word after the consonant. (A word family pattern should appear.)

lem/on   hab/it   cred/it

2. Practice with the words in Appendices H5 and H6.

Appendices H5 and H6 contain easy and hard words that follow the One-Consonant— Oops Rule.

The One-Consonant—Oops Rule

Sometimes the One-Consonant Rule does not work. When that happens, divide the word after the consonant. The vowel becomes short.

wag/on   vis/it   sec/ond   ov/en   trav/el

The Three Long-Word Rules Summarized

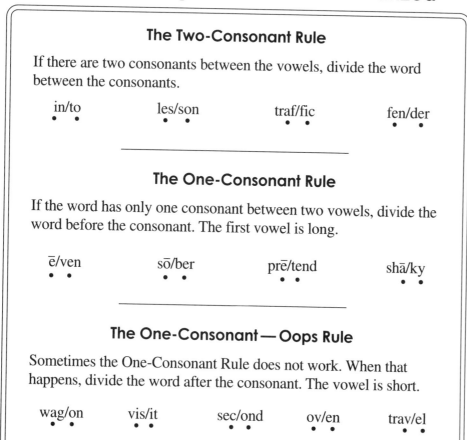

The Two-Consonant Rule

If there are two consonants between the vowels, divide the word between the consonants.

in/to   les/son   traf/fic   fen/der

The One-Consonant Rule

If the word has only one consonant between two vowels, divide the word before the consonant. The first vowel is long.

ē/ven   sō/ber   prē/tend   shā/ky

The One-Consonant — Oops Rule

Sometimes the One-Consonant Rule does not work. When that happens, divide the word after the consonant. The vowel is short.

wag/on   vis/it   sec/ond   ov/en   trav/el

Creating more rules would be counter-productive.

Important Notes:

The three long-word rules will not necessarily result in word divisions that match the dictionary. This is not the purpose of the rules. Instead, the long-word rules will help the student read the word. (For example, the dictionary divides the word *baker* as bak-er, which might be interpreted as "backer," while the long-word rules produce ba-ker, a form more helpful to the student.)

The three long-word rules will not cover all situations (such as three consonants or -LE at the end). It is possible to create more rules to cover more situations; however, this is counter-productive. Managing three rules is challenging enough. Given sufficient practice in only three rules, most students get the idea and begin seeing natural word divisions without making dots and drawing lines. At that point, the long-word rules can be dropped. The student will have outgrown them.

8 Writing

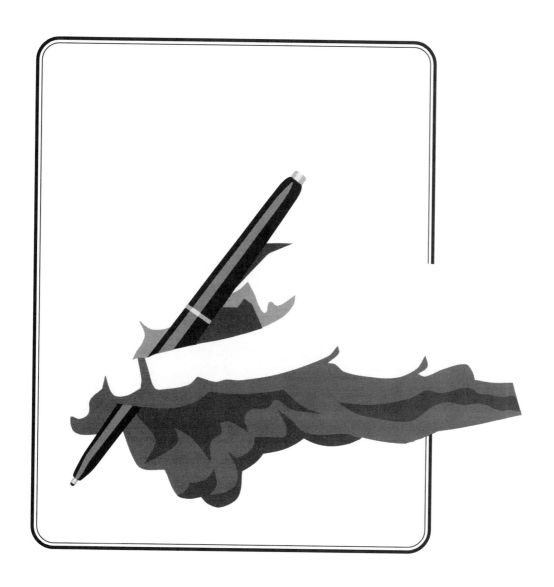

*"I hope to get a job if I work hard.
I have learned a lot of things.
I couldn't even write a letter
before I came."*
— George, an adult literacy student

Writing

This chapter will provide you with principles of teaching writing and with 11 strategies for teaching writing:

The Writing Part of the Lesson

Even if your student has no specific writing goals, you should still teach writing if only because many students experience *reading* improvement after beginning *writing* instruction. Writing instruction activates new reading skills by establishing new thinking patterns in the brain.

The phrase "learning to write" can mean learning:

- To print (manuscript writing).
- To write in cursive.
- To spell (included in the Word Study part of the lesson in LITSTART).
- To construct complete sentences with standard grammar, punctuation, and capitalization.

These are the mechanical, "left-brained" aspects of writing. "Learning to write" can also mean learning the creative "right-brained" aspects of writing:

- To construct short messages like a grocery list or a note for a spouse.
- To express casual, conversational thoughts comfortably as in a friendly letter or a journal.
- To develop accurate reports, proper business letters, or convincing essays with clear statements and logical organization.
- To express an exciting or moving story with calculated pacing and vivid images.

A Common Error

When tutors focus only on the mechanical aspects of writing, students learn those skills but often have trouble creating clear, natural-sounding paragraphs. Students become so focused on commas and penmanship that they lose the message. They sometimes develop a fear of writing.

Implications for tutoring:

Teach writing as a process, not a product. In other words, show your student how to get some ideas out on paper and how to manipulate them. Let your student experience writing as a free flow of thoughts without the fear of spelling errors. Correct the mechanics last, if at all.

Many students experience reading improvement after beginning writing instruction.

Writing Myths

Myths #1, #2, and #3:
Students must learn penmanship, spelling, and grammar before they can write.

Not necessarily. Read this:

> I hav brother. he liv in mie contre.
> he not marrid. I not se him 3 yeers. I
> want se him in may. I go see him and
> mi fother and mie mother. I stay 3
> weeks. I cum bak in Junn.

Don't
overcorrect.

Did the writer successfully communicate a thought to you?

If the writer transferred thoughts on paper to you, then the writer was successful. The purpose of writing is to communicate.

While spelling, penmanship, and grammar are important, the message is usually more important.

Implications for tutoring:

Let your student know that the message is more important than spelling, penmanship, or grammar. This may give your student the courage to actually use writing for anything from making a grocery list to leaving an important note for a family member.

When you review a writing exercise, show that you understand and value the message by commenting on and responding to the message ("That sounds wonderful! Does your brother live with your parents?") before correcting minor errors.

Don't overcorrect. Pick only a couple of errors or one general principle to work on, such as "remember to start with a capital letter."

Penmanship

Most adult students have a legible style of manuscript writing (printing) or cursive writing. If your student's penmanship is legible, do not spend valuable tutoring time trying to change it, unless:

- Your student has expressed a desire to develop better penmanship.

- Your student forms certain letters in a way that makes those particular letters difficult to read.

Principles of Adult Penmanship

- The goal for adult penmanship is *legibility,* not conformity.

- Penmanship style is a matter of personal choice; many people modify the "textbook" style. The student should be the final judge of what is "good enough" or what is appealing.

Tips on Teaching Penmanship

- Let the student select from various models (some samples are in Appendix N). Backhand or a printing style is fine.

- If your student has trouble controlling the letters, try using paper with extra guidelines.

- Make sure the student's forearm is on the table for good control.

- Correct specific problems by explaining why the correction is important, practicing a bit, and then reminding the student periodically.

Grammar

Many tutors wonder about whether to correct their students' grammar, both in speaking and in writing. The first step in exploring this question is to avoid thinking of grammar in terms of good, bad, proper, or improper. It is not a moral issue.

Different Styles of Grammar

It may be helpful to think in terms of different styles of grammar. There is an academic/business/official grammar known as standard grammar. Then there are various styles of street/ethnic/regional grammar, known collectively as nonstandard grammar. Some people can shift between different styles of grammar for different situations. All styles of grammar have rules. The rules may not be written, but they are there.

Some elements of nonstandard grammar are actually clearer, more democratic, or more expressive than standard grammar. The meaning of "y'all" is clearer than "you." "It do" is intrinsically better than "it does" because it is consistent with "I do," "you do," and "they do" and because it is therefore easier to learn.

This is not to encourage nonstandard grammar, but rather to encourage at least a tolerance of your student's grammar and perhaps even an appreciation for the cultural beauty that it represents. Some students cherish the grammar that represents their cultural identity. Other students want to change their grammar to prepare for a new job or higher education.

Students of English as a second language usually adopt the grammar used at work or in their community. See page 76 for other notes on ESL grammar.

The Solution

The final answer, then, to the question, "Should I correct my student's grammar?" is: ask your student. If your student wants to work on grammar or if standard grammar would clearly help achieve the student's goal, do it; otherwise, don't.

If you do decide to work on grammar, pick one issue to tackle at a time. See pages 8 and 10 for guidelines.

Avoid thinking of grammar in terms of good, bad, proper, or improper.

Spelling

Contrary to logic, a person does not have to be able to spell well before being able to write complete thoughts on paper. In fact, it is preferable for adult students to write real thoughts right from the beginning. Adults cannot afford to wait for perfect spelling when they have immediate writing needs.

How is it possible to write without being able to spell? Three elements are key:

- The strategy of temporary spelling (Strategy 50), which states that if a writer has something to say and does not know how to spell it, it is okay to just spell a word the way it sounds in order to get the thought on paper. Later, the spelling can be corrected if need be.

- The support of a tutor in using temporary spelling, so that such efforts are seen not as bad spelling but as good writing. Have faith that, just as people learn to dance by starting with awkward steps, people can learn to write by starting with awkward spelling. Improvement comes naturally with practice and gentle guidance.

- The inclusion of traditional spelling instruction as a separate part of the lesson so that temporary spelling becomes less and less necessary. With experience, you will be able to use patterns that you notice in your student's temporary spelling to create spelling lessons for the Word Study portion of the lesson.

Adult students who use temporary spelling find that almost instantly they have the power to make lists, to leave a note for a spouse, to record important information, to preserve memories, and even to draft letters to public officials if they want to. The students have a motto: **If you can say it, you can write it.**

Strategies 51-60 can be used to help your student with writing. Temporary spelling can be used in all of them.

Temporary spelling is not bad spelling but good writing.

Strategy 50

Temporary Spelling

Uses:

- To empower the student to be able to put virtually any thought on paper.

- To reduce fear of writing.

- As a tool for Strategies 51, 52, 54, 57-60.

"If you can say it, you can write it."

Procedure:

1. Explain that a few hundred years ago, there were no dictionaries and people often invented their own spelling. Two people might spell the same word differently.

2. Suggest that this old method can often be used when a person does not know how to spell a word. Drawings and blank lines can also be used. The important thing is to get the idea out on paper. The spelling can always be changed later.

3. Encourage temporary spelling in concert with other writing strategies (especially 51, 52, 54, 57-60). Spelling can be fixed when the writing is completed or not at all.

Tip:

Watch for patterns in the student's temporary spelling to find ideas for later spelling instruction. Teach spelling as a separate subject (Chapter 7).

orung joos for br--f--s

O J 4 bkfs

ornj j——— for berckfus

ⓘ juse for brikfust

Everyday Scenarios

Strategy 51

Uses:
- To motivate the student to write.
- To provide practice in writing for real-life situations.

Procedure:
1. Ask your student to select a real-life writing scenario to practice (see side column for ideas).
2. If possible, show a simple example of the item.
3. With your student, create a writing scenario from the student's life, such as:
    - You are going to the store. Your son will be home soon and won't know where you are.
    - You want to remember to call your sister on her birthday.
4. Support the student in deciding what to write. Encourage the student to use temporary spelling* (Strategy 50) with little assistance from you.
5. Ask the student to read the item aloud.
6. Encourage the student to actually use the item for its stated purpose.

* Correct the spelling if the student wishes, but note that most items serve their purpose without being corrected. Minimizing corrections encourages the student to use writing for real life.

Use this strategy for:

Calendar entries

Cathartic letters (to vent emotions, not to send)

Directions (travel)

Journals

Drafts of important items

Instructions (how-to)

Letters to family*

Letters to friends*

Lists:
  Shopping
  To-do
  Gift ideas
  Goals
  Birthdays/anniversaries
  Packing
  Phone numbers
  Inventory

Quick notes to family

Recipes

Phone messages

Reminder notes to self

178

Strategy 52

Written Conversation

Uses:
- To provide writing practice in a casual framework.
- To provide an opportunity for the student to learn from the tutor's model.

Procedure:

1. Explain to the student that you will try to have a conversation on paper. Explain that spelling will not matter for this exercise. The student should just spell the words the way they sound (Strategy 50).

2. Begin by writing a question or comment. Pass the note to your student and ask your student to respond in writing and pass the note back to you.

3. Respond only to the content, as you would in a conversation. Do not correct spelling or other errors unless your student asks a specific question.

4. When possible, incorporate in your responses words that your student has misspelled. Your student might use some of your words as models.

5. Silently note patterns in the student's errors. Use these patterns to determine future spelling exercises.

What did you do today?

I bay sitd to daey
My grannd kites
I wths vree hape.

How many grandkids
do you have?
How old are they?
I bet you make
them very happy too!

I have to grandkids
They are to grols They
are ow and to years
old and am a vaery
hap grand dad.

This authentic excerpt from a Written Conversation illustrates:

- How a student, without prompting, might use the tutor's message as a resource to correct his own spelling (grandkids).

- That incorrect spelling (very happy) is not reinforced by incorrect temporary spelling. It is a new invention each time.

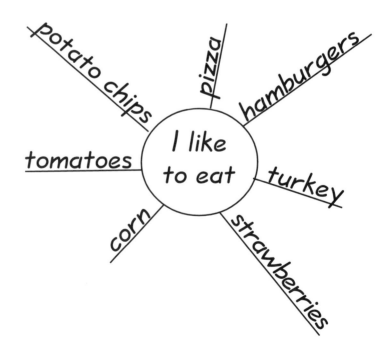

//////// **Strategy 53**

Guided Writing (Beginning)

Uses: To allow a beginning-level student to experience success with writing.

Procedure:
1. With the student, select a topic and write it in the form of an incomplete sentence in a circle.

2. Ask the student to supply possible words to complete the sentence. Write the responses on rays, creating a basic story map.

3. Have the student write a story using the map for reference.

4. Ask the student to read the new story.

Possible topics:

My daughter is ...

I wish I could buy ...

On weekends I ...

At work I ...

I like to ...

I wish I could ...

I wish I had more ...

Dogs can be ...

My mother used to ...

My kitchen ...

Last Saturday I ...

June 23

I like to eat pizza.

I like to eat tomatoes.

I like to eat turkey.

I like to eat hamburgers.

I like to eat corn.

I like to eat strawberries.

I like to eat potato chips.

Strategy 54

Guided Writing (Intermediate and Advanced)

Uses: For the intermediate or advanced student to experience success with writing.

Procedure:

1. Help the student select a topic and write it in a circle.

2. Ask the student to supply words that come to mind about the topic. Write the words on rays, grouping related words as shown. (If your student is advanced, transfer the responsibility for Step 2 to your student after demonstrating this strategy a few times.)

3. Show the student how to use the words on a selected ray to create an oral sentence and transfer the sentence to paper. Give the pen to the student and help the student continue the process with another ray. (Deviate from the map if the student wishes.) Offer guidance but avoid rewording the student's natural sentences.

4. Ask the student to read the composition.

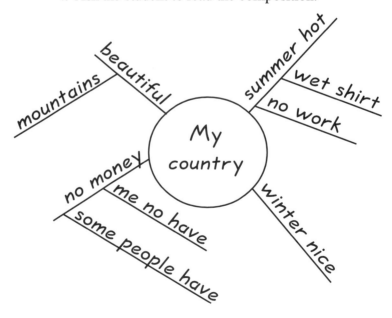

In my country is very beautiful. The mountains is very beautiful. In my country is very hot. In summer my shirt is wet. Too hot for working. In winter is nice. No need coats. In my country people is very nice. But some people is not nice. In my country people no have much money. But some people have money. Not me.

Strategy 55

Dictated Sentences

Uses:
- To reinforce spelling skills.
- To teach basic capitalization and punctuation.
- To provide left-brained students with a structured method for easing into writing activities (should build up to activities using temporary spelling).

Procedure:
1. After the student practices spelling words using any strategy from 37 to 41, ask the student to write the sentences that you will dictate.

2. Make up a few sentences (just 3 or 4 at first) that:
   - are short and simple.
   - use words from the spelling list of the day (such as the -OT family pattern illustrated) and, if possible, other words from recent spelling exercises.
   - often relate to the student's life and include the names of the student's family or friends.
   - sound conversational, not contrived, even if the sentence includes difficult words (just supply the spelling as needed).

3. Repeat the sentence and help the student with spelling, capitalization, and punctuation as needed. (This is not a test; it is practice.)

> I did <u>not</u> see the show.
> We did a <u>lot</u> of work today.
> Chris <u>got</u> a new job.
> It is <u>not</u> too <u>hot</u> today.

Variation:
Start a sentence and let the student create an ending. ("I did not see the _____.") Help with spelling as needed.

Assisted Writing — *Strategy 56*

Uses:

- To provide assistance with official paperwork.
- To provide guidance when the student wants to learn or meet customary standards.

Procedure:

1. If appropriate, use scrap paper or a copy of the item for practice before writing on the official paper.
2. Encourage the student to say aloud the first answer or sentence. Provide assistance as needed.
3. Invite the student to start writing while you help remember the response and assist with spelling.
4. Continue to the end with more responses or items.
5. If appropriate, help the student to revise and recopy the item.

Use this strategy for:

Applications

Checks

Envelopes

Forms

Greeting cards

Gift tags

Invitations

Note to child's teacher

Memos to co-workers

Thank-you notes

Sympathy notes

Workbook answers

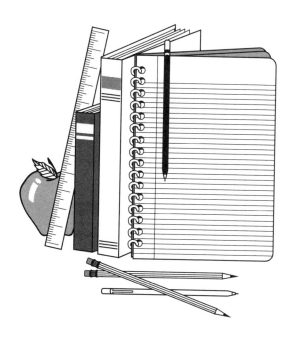

Strategy 57 Writing 1, 2, 3

cities

dogs

sports

baseball stars

fast food

soups

uncles

TV shows

houses

cars

fruit

shoes

tasks at work

child care

weekends

heroes

I wish

I love

I hate

I need

We should

Uses:
- To increase writing ease through practice.
- To provide a combination of structure and creativity in a writing exercise.

Procedure: Guide the student through the steps below, letting the student do as much of the work alone as possible. For a beginner, just do Steps 1 and 2.

1. Choose a general topic from a list. (Alternatively, let the student suggest a topic or draw a topic from a hat.) Write the topic on the top of a page (for example: sports).

2. List **three** specific examples of the topic (baseball, football, basketball). Use temporary spelling (Strategy 50).

3. Look at the **three** examples and think of some way that the **three** are all different or all the same. Write that in a sentence. (Baseball, football, and basketball all use a ball, but the balls are different.) This is the first sentence of your paragraph.

4. Under that sentence, write **three** more sentences, one for each example. (A baseball is small and hard. A football is long with a point on each end. A basketball is as large as a man's head.)

5. Intermediate students: You are done.

   _____

   Advanced students: Add detail to the **three** sentences to build **three** paragraphs about the **three** items.

6. Advanced students: Expand the initial sentence into a paragraph that previews your **three** middle paragraphs. Add a concluding paragraph that summarizes your paper. This strategy can be used as Steps 1 and 2 for Strategy 60.

Journal Writing

Strategy 58

Uses:
- To encourage writing at home.
- To increase writing ease through practice.
- To create a memento and measure of progress.

Procedure:

1. Provide a notebook and discuss the idea of writing a journal. The student can write on any topic—from a special event (I visited my sister today) to random thoughts (I hope my son improves his math). If no ideas arise, the student can describe the day's routine (I had soup for lunch).

2. Write a sample entry that is short and simple so that it provides an attainable model. Cross out words and use arrows to illustrate how to make changes.

3. Help the student write journal entries for a few weeks until the student is ready to try daily entries at home. Encourage temporary spelling (Strategy 50).

4. Read the student's journal. Respond to the *content*. Talk about the *ideas*. Ignore spelling errors (unless the student specifically asks for corrections).

Variation:

1. Use conversation to find a topic that is meaningful to the student. Write the topic at the top of a page.

2. Write about the topic in your journal for a few minutes while your student does the same.

3. Exchange journals and read each other's thoughts.

4. (Option: After trying this a few times, suggest that you could each write at home and then exchange journals at the next lesson.)

Strategy 59 Free Writing

Uses:
- To overcome fear of writing and increase writing fluency.

- To serve as a basis for letters, essays, or reports (see Strategy 60).

Procedure: 1. Agree with your student that you will both write for five minutes according to these rules:

- Start writing immediately and never stop until time is up.

- Write whatever is in your mind.

- If you don't know how to spell it, fake it.

- If you can't think of what to write, just write "I can't think of what to say" as many times as you want.

- Never stop to look back, cross anything out, or decide which word to use. Keep writing always.

2. When time is up, read what you wrote. Do not criticize or change your writing. Do not correct errors. Free writing is free.

3. (Option: Underline your favorite thoughts from your free writing. Use these new topics to start another free write or to start a more structured writing activity, such as Strategy 53, 54, or 57.)

I cant think of what to write about but I shoud probbly write something. I wish I could write better. it is so hard to spell. I reelly have troubul when I have to leave a messej for someboddy expeshally at work. One time I

Process Writing   *Strategy 60*

Uses: For thoughtful or formal writing.

Procedure: Guide the student through the steps below, letting the student do as much of the work as possible. Skip Step 1 if the words flow freely. Stop after Step 2, 3, or 4 if the purpose of the writing warrants it.

1. **Pre-write** (find some words to get started).
   - Talk it out with a friend, or
   - Dictate thoughts into a tape recorder, or
   - Brainstorm, or
   - Free write (Strategy 59), or
   - Make a map (Strategy 54), or
   - Make a list (Strategy 57).

2. Make a **sloppy copy** (first draft) from the words generated in Step 1.
   - Write on every other line or on a computer.
   - Focus on ideas, not mechanics.
   - Make it messy: use carets, temporary spelling (Strategy 50), arrows, and scribbles.

3. **Revise** for content only (not mechanics).
   - Read it aloud, thinking of the audience.
   - Look for parts that are confusing, unrelated to the topic, incomplete, or out of sequence.
   - Get suggestions from others.
   - Rewrite (perhaps on computer).

4. **Proofread** for grammar, spelling, and punctuation.
   - Get comments from others.
   - Check a dictionary and other resources.
   - Use spelling and grammar checks if writing on a computer.

5. **Share** your final, neat copy.
   - Give it or send it to a friend or official, or
   - Post it on a bulletin board, or
   - Send it to a newspaper or newsletter.

Use this strategy for:

Course assignments

Competitions

Essays

Family history

Fiction

Letters
> *to friends*
> *to relatives*
> *to pen pals*
> *to public officials*
> *to the editor*
> *complaints*
> *requests*

Memoirs

Newsletter articles

Poetry

Practice writing

9

Checking Progress

"I've learned more in the last two years than I have in my whole life."

--- Tanya, an adult literacy student

Checking Progress

This chapter will provide some ideas for keeping track of the progress that your student makes:

Measuring Progress

Your student needs to see progress in order to maintain motivation. You, as the tutor, need to check progress periodically to maintain your own motivation and to evaluate your tutoring strategies.

Often, the progress is self-evident. You and your student can see it and feel it at almost every session. At other times, you may not be sure, or it may seem that the student is not progressing. Actually, it is likely that the progress is there but it hasn't been documented.

There are several ways to document or monitor your progress.

Mini-Goals

Help your student set **attainable** mini-goals, such as:

> I will meet two hours a week for ten weeks.
> I will finish this book by June 1.
> I will say hello to my neighbor in English next week.
> I will write ten Experience Stories.
> I will learn to spell this list of words.

Write the goals down, date them, and check them off or give yourselves a reward when you attain a goal.

Portfolios

Try keeping a portfolio (see next page).

Formal Assessment

Perhaps your literacy organization provides pre- and post-testing services. Such testing might confirm your student's progress and renew your motivation. Be aware, however, that it is possible for a student to learn many skills and yet show no progress on a test. If this is the case, rely on mini-goals and the portfolio (next page) for a more personalized assessment. (Note that the *Where To Start* Placement Guide that accompanies this book is not a test and is not designed to show progress.)

Help your student set attainable mini-goals.

Portfolios

One way for you and your student to keep track of your progress is to keep a portfolio. A portfolio is simply an envelope, a folder, or a box that contains samples of the student's work and other evidence of progress.

Every few months, you and your student can review the portfolio, compare new work with old, update information, reflect on accomplishments, and modify plans.

The portfolio belongs to the student. It remains in the student's possession and the student decides what goes into and comes out of the portfolio.

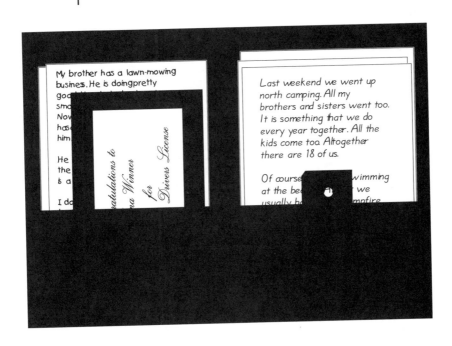

Sample Contents of a Portfolio

Goal Setting
- Initial goal statement
- Checklist of steps toward goals
- Records of progress toward goals

Speaking
- Tapes of answers to same questions at different dates
- Samples of notes, word lists, and other pages from notebook

Reading
- Audio tape of reading of the same material every 2 to 3 months
- Analysis of improvements noted on tape (fewer errors, greater fluency, better expression)
- Log of milestones in reading (first story, first complete book, first newspaper article, first recipe, first greeting card)
- List of books and other materials read
- Log of items read outside of class (labels, TV book, road signs)

Writing
- Samples of writing
- Analysis of improvements noted in writing samples
- Log of milestones in writing (first grocery list, first complete sentence, first paragraphs, first journal entry with perfect spelling, first letter mailed, first full-page story)
- Copies of the above milestone items
- Journals
- Spelling lists or tests

Other Information
- Log of feelings about reading (confidence, anxiety, interest)
- Tutor's log
- Student's log
- Log of extra work done at home
- Attendance record
- Certificates, awards
- Miscellaneous anecdotes
- Formal test results
- Photos and other mementos
- Anything else of significance to student

Date everything in the portfolio.

Maintaining Motivation

Everyone has a bad day now and then, but if your student seems to be getting genuinely discouraged, it's your job to tune in to the problem and look for a solution:

- Try more praise.
- Try easier work for a while.
- Try fewer corrections.
- Keep a positive attitude yourself.
- Add humor.
- Suggest that the student get involved with activities with other students.
- Look for inspirational models, perhaps another student who has succeeded or a story about a person who has overcome hardships.
- Have a candid talk with the student. Ask for the source of the discouragement. Talk together about how to correct it.
- If the student is experiencing problems at home or work, use the problem for conversation (ESL), for an Experience Story, or for cathartic writing. Look for reading material related to the problem.
- Ask other tutors or your literacy coordinator for suggestions.
- Try some different strategies or a different book.
- Take a fun day. Play some word games or go on a field trip.
- Bring in a treat.
- Help the student start a list of accomplishments.
- Give the student a certificate.
- Build up that portfolio.

Transitions

At some point your lesson routine may need to be modified. Your student will either finish the book, master the skills, or achieve identified goals, or perhaps you will both be ready for a change. This is a good time to check the student's portfolio, re-evaluate goals, find new materials, or experiment with new activities. Include your student in these planning decisions.

When your student reaches a milestone, it is a time to rejoice. Acknowledge this progress with a certificate of achievement and a shower of praise. Every ounce of pride translates to future motivation.

If the achievement represents the student's ultimate goal, celebrate this special occasion together. Talk to your student about next steps. Notify your literacy coordinator of the student's success.

If your student has reached the top of the basic literacy scale, perhaps you can inspire your student to pursue more education in adult high school, a trade school, or college. Maybe a new job, some community service, or even a new hobby can provide the next challenge. Learning is a lifelong process. Encourage your student to build on success.

And, by the way, congratulations to you, too!

This

Certificate of Achievement

is presented to

Kim Lillie

for

Voting for the first time

Congratulations
and best wishes for continued success

Presented by _Joan Martin_   Date_Nov. 5_

Appendices

"I am doing things today that I would never have thought of doing. Every day life is easier"

--- Robert, an adult literacy student

Appendices

Appendix A:
Consonant Word Lists

B b

baseball & bat*
bunt
beer
book
Bible
boy
baby
bottle
bowling
basketball
boxing
birthday
bird
bills
beef
bumblebee
bone

C c

cat
coffee
car
Coke
curve*
cop
cash
cool
cucumber
cave*
cocoa
cup*
cow
catcher's mitt*
corn
Canada
coach

D d

dog
dance
dinner
dish
dad
daughter
dollars
dime
date
day
dynamite
dud
delicious
dinosaur
diamond
dive
deer

F f

football
field goal
feather
finger
fork*
food
fat
fish
fudge
family
father
fun
February
fool
fall
fashion
foot

G g

go
guy
girl
gas
gun
gift
guard
gamble
good
gang
gold
game
garden
garage
gum
gate
goose

H h

husband
hurricane
hamburger
hammer
hand
home
home run
hockey
heaven
hell
high
house
hot
hunter
hair
hunk
honey

J j

job
junk
Jello
jump shot*
jail
judge
jewelry*
jeep
juice
jumbo jet
January
June
July
joker
jam
jacket
Japan

K k

king
key
kiss
kite
kitchen
kid
kick
kicker*
karate
kangaroo
kitten
ketchup
kidney
kind
keep
kill
kindergarten

See Strategies 26 and 27 for ideas for using these words.

* The starred words suggest a picture that looks like the letter. For example, the letter C looks like a **c**urve—a good memory trick. Some words, like "kicker," use the letter twice.

© 1999 Michigan Literacy, Inc.

L l

lady
lucky
love
long line*
landlord
landlady
little
liquor
lake
log*
lunch
ladder
lottery
leg*
labor
leaf
luxury

M m

mountain*
money
man
muscles
machine
mother
mom
movies
music
mumps*
mustard
McDonald's*
microwave
Monday
makeup
magazine
Mexico

N n

no
nickel
nail
news
navy
neck
never
nose
net
north
noon
nice
nothing
needle
needlenose
neighbor
nine

P p

penny
pots and pans*
pepper
puppy
paper
paycheck
police
pink
purple
piano
pitcher
pig
pipe
pinball
people
potato
party

Q q

queen
quarter
quarterback
quarrel
question
quart
quilt
quit
quiz
quiet
quicksand
quality
quake
quack
queasy
quail
quadruplets

R r

railroad
river
road
rock
radio
rich
red
rat
read
restroom
rainbow
rocket
race
runner
rally
rain
referee

S s

snake*
sausage
soap
snowstorm
Sunday
sister
sale
summer
September
skater
south
silver
salt
sixty-six
sun
son
sing a song

T t

table*
telescope
telephone
toilet
touchdown
tornado
tie
tent
tiptoe
tea
tall
tail
teeth
tunnel
Tuesday
tomato
terrible

* The starred words suggest a picture that looks like the letter. For example, the letter S looks like a snake (and coincidentally, makes the sound of a snake).

V v

video
valley*
valentine
vest*
van
vitamin
vet
volcano*
vacuum
vanilla
volleyball
vegetable
vine
vacant
vinegar
veil
velvet

W w

woman
wet
waves*
wash
worm
wine
winter
wife
winner
weekend
work
water
wood
Wednesday
wonderful
World War I
witch

X x

*The words below **end** with the sound of X.*

box
tax
ax
six
mix
fix
fax
ox
fox
sax
sex
wax
pox
ex
max

Y y

yes
yellow
yesterday
yet
yard
yarn
young
yam
yeast
year
yolk
yogurt
yell
yield
yardstick
yo-yo
yahoo

Z z

zigzag*
zoo
zebra
zero
zeal
zipper
zone
zap
zest
zucchini
zoom
zodiac
zenith
zinc
zip code
zany
zillion

* The starred words suggest a picture that looks like the letter. For example, the letter Z makes a zigzag pattern—a good memory trick for some students.

Appendix B:
Blend and Digraph Word Lists

*The L-Blends,
R-Blends, and
W-Blends*

See page 130 for
a definition of
blends.

See Strategies 26
and 27 for ideas
for using these
words.

bl

blood
blind
bluff
blue
black
bless
blade
blow
blizzard
blossom
blast
blond
blister
blame
bleach
blush

cl

clean
cling
clay
clap
close
clothes
closet
clip
climb
clock
clumsy
clue
class
cliff
cloth
clinic

dw

dwell
dwelling
dwindle
dwarf
Dwight
Dwayne

fl

fly
flakes
flee
flame
flag
flap
flat
flow
flu
flare
fling
flavor
flakes
flight
flower
flute

br

branch
brain
breath
brook
broad
break
broil
breakfast
broken
bread
bran
brave
braid
bride
bronze
brown

cr

cracker
crumbs
crazy
craft
creative
crayon
crust
creek
creeper
cry
crisis
croak
crucial
crank
crane
crawl

dr

drapes
drive
drove
dream
dress
drag
dryer
dragon
drip dry
drums
drink
draft
drama
dread
drunk
drown

fr

France
French
fries
freedom
fruit
friend
fresh
frog
freeze
frozen
frost
from
Friday
frame
free
frown

gl

glad
glory
glee
glide
glow
glue
glass
glossy
glance
glamor
glaze
glitter
gloves
globe

pl

play
plan
plastic
plywood
plow
plum
please
plate
place
pliers
plane
plague
planet
plank

tw

twin
twelve
twenty
twice
twine
twist
twister
twirl
tweezers
twilight
twinkle
twig

gr

grapes
greed
gravy
grow
gravity
great
greetings
gripe
groan
group
grease
grateful
gravel
ground
grill
Greece
Greek

pr

prince
princess
private
property
practice
praise
pretty
preacher
prime
problem
program
profession
promise
pray
proof
prune
prize

tr

truck
train
trailer
tractor
tree
treat
trip
tribe
trouble
troops
trim
truth
travel
trivia
trick
trespass
trillion

206

sc

scale
scarf
score
scat
scatter
scar
scan
scam
scary
scorch
scab
scoop
Scotland
scout

sk

skate
ski
skill
skillet
skeleton
sketch
skin
skinny
sky
skirt
skirmish
skid
skull
skunk

sl

slip
slide
sleep
sly
slick
sleigh
sling
sleeve
slice
slacks
slap
slang
slow
sled

sm

smell
smile
smoke
smart
small
smooch
smuggle
smooth
smash
smog
smack
smother
smudge
smear

sn

sneakers
snow
snooze
snake
sneeze
snap
snail
snore
snip
sneaky
snob
snoop
sniff
sniffle

sp

spark
spare
spirit
Spanish
Spain
spade
speak
spit
spider
sponge
speed
spin
spinach
spoil

squ

square
squeeze
squash
squat
squirrel
squeak
squad
squint
squaw
squabble
squawk
squeal
squirm
squirt

st

state
sting
stay
stone
staff
stereo
stain
steam
store
stop
steer
stove
stadium
stamp

sw

swing
swim
swear
sweat
swallow
swimmer
swan
swish
sweet
swine
swat
Swiss
Switzerland
Sweden

The S-Blends

scr

scream
screen
scram
scratch
scramble
scrape
screw
script
scrub

spl

splash
splendid
splinter
splint
split
splurge
splatter
spleen
splice

spr

sprain
spring
spread
sprinkle
spruce
sprocket
sprite
spray
sprout

str

string
street
stripe
strike
straight
strawberry
strap
strategy
strainer

Digraphs

ch

chair
chain
change
children
check
chin
chest
church
chapel
China
Chinese
cheek
cheer
cheese
chicken
choo-choo
chore
charge
cheat

sh

shoe
she
short
shut
shell
ship
shall
shirt
show
shovel
shower
shout
sharp
sheep
shelf
shift
shin
shine
shortstop

th*

the
that
this
their
these
them

three
thirty
thing
third
thumb
thunder
thigh
thick
thought
thank
Thanksgiving
Thursday

ph

phantom
phase
pharmacy
pharmacist
pheasant
philosophy
phone
phony
photo
photograph
phonics
phrase
physical
physician
phlox
Phil
Philip
Philippines
Phyllis

wh*

white
where
what
when
which
why
wheel
while
whether
whistle

shr**

shrink
shrub
shrimp
shrine
shrug
shriek
shrill
shred
shrewd
shrivel

thr**

three
thrifty
throw
threw
thread
throat
throne
through
thrill
thrash

* See page 131 for special information on the sounds of TH and WH.
** TheSHR and THR are technically R-blends that include digraphs.

See page 131 for a definition of digraphs.

See Strategies 26 and 27 for ideas for using these words.

Appendix C: Vowel Word Lists

Short Vowel Words

These words may help students hear or remember the short vowel sounds. The words can be used with Strategies 26 and 27.

Short A	Short E	Short I	Short O	Short U
apple	echo	itch	October	umbrella
answer	end	in	octopus	umpire
ant	exit	is	olive	unlucky
afternoon	exercise	it	opportunity	ugly
ad	entertain	inch	operation	uncle
animal	engine	igloo	optical	under
axle	elevator	interception	object	understand
actor	escalator	infield	occupation	underline
actress	elephant	inning	octane	undercoat
ask	elk	injury	opposite	underdog
ashes	exciting	industry	ox	underground
activity	edge	intermission	oxygen	underwater
antelope	enemy	illegal	optimist	us
Africa	education	ill	otter	unhappy
admiral	everybody	interesting	odd	umpteen
absent	ebony	icky	omelette	up
accent	entrance	ignition	Ontario	upset
accident	elm	insane	Oliver	uphill
avenue	expect	intelligent	̷honest	upstairs
avalanche	elbow	Inuit	̷honor	uppercut
athlete	Eskimo	Illinois	Oslo	usher
attic	Ed	Indiana	Ottawa	udder
attitude	Ellen	Italy	Oxford	ulcer
action	Edison	Indian	Ozzie	uh...
antenna	Emily	Israel	Osh Kosh	um...

Most readers do not know all the vowel sounds; they don't have to.

See pages 132-133 for an overview of vowels.

See Strategies 26 and 27 for ideas for using these words.

Long Vowel Words

Long A	Long E	Long I	Long O	Long U
able	each	I	open	use
ace	eat	iron	ocean	unit
ache	easy	ivy	over	unity
acre	east	item	omit	unify
aide	eel	idea	owe	union
aim	eaves	ice	oatmeal	uniform
age	eavesdrop	icicle	own	unison
agent	ether	iceberg	obey	unicorn
agency	even	ice cream	oak	unicycle
ale	evening	idle	odor	unilateral
alien	either	iodine	oath	useless
angel	ego	identical	oasis	universe
ape	eager	ivory	omen	ukulele
apron	eagle	iris	only	university
ate	easel	island	oleo	utensil
ancient	equal	identification	opium	unique
acorn	e-mail	isolation	oh!	unite
AWOL	evil	Ida	ozone	utility
ailment	Easter	Idaho	opal	utopia
ain't	Eli	Iowa	overseas	usual
Amy	Eve	Iceland	Oklahoma	United States
Ajax	Eden	Ireland	Ohio	Utah
April	Egypt	Irish	Otis	Unitarian
Asia	Ethiopia	Irene	Omaha	Ukraine
Abraham	Edith	Isaac	Ozarks	Utica

R-Controlled Vowel Words

er	ir	ur	ar	or
Ernest	irk	urge	arm	or
Erma	Irving	urgent	army	organ
---------	---------	urn	artist	orange
her	fir	urban	arch	orchestra
sister	girl	--------	archery	ornament
brother	bird	fur	Arctic	orient
mother	girdle	furniture	argue	Oregon
father	sir	burn	------------	orchard
fern	stir	turn	car	ornery
fertilizer	dirt	murmur	far	----------
member	fir	rural	farm	for
Germany	firm	purse	bar	forty
serve	first	nurse	barn	horrible
service	birch	jury	bark	corn
serpent	birthday	turkey	charge	born
percent	shirt	flurries	darling	morning
person	skirt	turtle	alarm	porch
perch	flirt	hurt	card	north
perfect	sirloin	burp	party	Norway
sherbet	squirt	splurge	park	Florida
certain	squirrel	hurry	pardon	New York
germs	whirl	curl	garden	gorgeous
sterling	swirl	survey	garbage	lord
termite	twirl	surface	market	short
merchandise	thirty	Thursday	star	snore
thermometer	thirsty	turf	sharp	storm
jerk	circus	turpentine	marshal	shore
perk	circle	blurry	marble	story
clerk	third	during	smart	sport

Words with Two R-Controlled Vowels

farmer	border	murder	Arthur	perjury
farther	corner	burger		
garter	order	further		
barber				

Words with Other Vowel Sounds

aw	**short o͝o**	**oi**	**ou**
awful	book	oil	ouch
awkward	good	oink	out
awe	cook	point	our
awesome	stood	joint	sour
law	crook	boil	loud
lawn	shook	coil	proud
claw	foot	coin	shout
paw	hood	join	south
pawn	took	toilet	mouth
raw		choice	house
saw	**long o͞o**	rejoice	mouse
slaw		sirloin	mountain
straw	moon	soil	sound
thaw	broom	spoil	ground
fawn	school	Detroit	found
yawn	food		hour
	boot	**oy**	scout
au	goof		
	goose	boy	**ow**
auction	loose	toy	
August	tooth	Roy	how
author	shoot	soy	now
autumn	booth	oyster	brown
automatic	noon	joyful	cow
Australia	moose	boycott	down
cause	rooster	enjoy	town
sauce	soon	employ	frown
saucer	proof	annoy	crowd
sausage	spoon	decoy	towel
taught	poodle	royal	vowel
caught	voodoo	loyal	shower
fault		destroy	tower

Appendix D:
Vowel Sounds

The Many Voices of A

Vowel sounds can vary in different parts of the country.

(See page 132.)

1. **Short A:** See pages 132, 133, and 208.

2. **Long A:** See pages 132, 133, and 209. The cues for long A are AI (wait, mail), AY (day, stay), A_E (make, paste), and A at the end of a syllable (A•pril, pa•per, ta•ble).

3. **Short O:** The A can sometimes sound like a **short O** (*ah*) (father, yacht, cha cha, macho).

4. **Short U or schwa:** The A sometimes sounds like a **short U** (*uh*) in a multi-syllable word (about, America, woman, Canada). Although this sound is technically a schwa (a brief, unaccented *uh* sound shown in dictionaries as an upside-down e [ə]), it is usually best taught to literacy students as a short U sound or perhaps mispronounced as a short A (jubilant) to help with spelling.

5. **Other:** In a few cases, the A by itself can sound like another vowel:
   • **Short E**: (any, many, said, says)
   • **Short I**: (message, salvage, terrace)

6. **Silent A:** The A is **silent** in the combinations EA and OA (team, coat).

7. **AU and AW:** AU is used for the middle of the word (audio, Paul); AW is used for the end of the word (law) or for the end of a root word before a suffix (awful, awesome).

8. **AR:** The AR usually sounds like the AR in car, but it can also sound like **ER** (blizzard, hazard) or like **AIR** (parent, carry, various).

9. **AIR and ARE:** Although this sound is often grouped with the long A's, it is technically different (fair, pair, care, glare).

10. **AL:** The A usually sounds like **AU** when followed by L (talk, all, walnut). (In the -ALK combination, the L is silent.)

11. **WA:** The A usually sounds like a **short O** (*ah*) or an **AU** (depending on the speaker's accent) when preceded by W (water, wash, want).

12. **WAR:** The combination WAR sounds like **WOR** (warm, warrant).

13. **Exceptions:** There are always exceptions: have (contradicts item 2), wax (contradicts item 11), laugh (contradicts item 7), forward (contradicts item 12), and so on.

There are no strategies for using this information because it is intended for your reference only.

Words with Other Vowel Sounds

aw
awful
awkward
awe
awesome
law
lawn
claw
paw
pawn
raw
saw
slaw
straw
thaw
fawn
yawn

au
auction
August
author
autumn
automatic
Australia
cause
sauce
saucer
sausage
taught
caught
fault

short o͝o
book
good
cook
stood
crook
shook
foot
hood
took

long o͞o
moon
broom
school
food
boot
goof
goose
loose
tooth
shoot
booth
noon
moose
rooster
soon
proof
spoon
poodle
voodoo

oi
oil
oink
point
joint
boil
coil
coin
join
toilet
choice
rejoice
sirloin
soil
spoil
Detroit

oy
boy
toy
Roy
soy
oyster
joyful
boycott
enjoy
employ
annoy
decoy
royal
loyal
destroy

ou
ouch
out
our
sour
loud
proud
shout
south
mouth
house
mouse
mountain
sound
ground
found
hour
scout

ow
how
now
brown
cow
down
town
frown
crowd
towel
vowel
shower
tower

Appendix D: Vowel Sounds

The Many Voices of A

Vowel sounds can vary in different parts of the country.

(See page 132.)

1. **Short A:** See pages 132, 133, and 208.

2. **Long A:** See pages 132, 133, and 209. The cues for long A are AI (wait, mail), AY (day, stay), A_E (make, paste), and A at the end of a syllable (A•pril, pa•per, ta•ble).

3. **Short O:** The A can sometimes sound like a **short O** (*ah*) (father, yacht, cha cha, macho).

4. **Short U or schwa:** The A sometimes sounds like a **short U** (*uh*) in a multi-syllable word (about, America, woman, Canada). Although this sound is technically a schwa (a brief, unaccented *uh* sound shown in dictionaries as an upside-down e [ə]), it is usually best taught to literacy students as a short U sound or perhaps mispronounced as a short A (jubilant) to help with spelling.

5. **Other:** In a few cases, the A by itself can sound like another vowel:
   • **Short E**: (any, many, said, says)
   • **Short I**: (message, salvage, terrace)

6. **Silent A:** The A is **silent** in the combinations EA and OA (team, coat).

7. **AU and AW:** AU is used for the middle of the word (audio, Paul); AW is used for the end of the word (law) or for the end of a root word before a suffix (awful, awesome).

8. **AR:** The AR usually sounds like the AR in car, but it can also sound like **ER** (blizzard, hazard) or like **AIR** (parent, carry, various).

9. **AIR and ARE:** Although this sound is often grouped with the long A's, it is technically different (fair, pair, care, glare).

10. **AL:** The A usually sounds like **AU** when followed by L (talk, all, walnut). (In the -ALK combination, the L is silent.)

11. **WA:** The A usually sounds like a **short O** (*ah*) or an **AU** (depending on the speaker's accent) when preceded by W (water, wash, want).

12. **WAR:** The combination WAR sounds like **WOR** (warm, warrant).

13. **Exceptions:** There are always exceptions: have (contradicts item 2), wax (contradicts item 11), laugh (contradicts item 7), forward (contradicts item 12), and so on.

There are no strategies for using this information because it is intended for your reference only.

CAUTION: As these pages indicate, the sounds for vowels are complex. This appendix should not be used as a basis for teaching vowels but merely to answer questions that might arise. See page 132 for guidance on teaching vowels.

The Many Voices of E

1. **Short E:** See pages 132, 133, and 208.

2. **Long E:** See pages 132, 133, and 209. The cues for long E are EA (sea, meat, weak), EE (see, meet, week), E_E (Pete), and E at the end of a syllable (e•ven, fe•ver, me).

3. **EA** and **EAD:** Instead of the expected long E, the EA sometimes sounds like a **short E** (breakfast, heaven, measure), especially in the combination EAD (head, thread, ready). The EA can also sound like a **long A** (steak, great).

4. **Short U** or **schwa:** The E sometimes sounds like a **short U** (*uh*) in a multi-syllable word (women, item, diet). Although this sound is technically a schwa (a brief *uh* sound shown in dictionaries as an upside-down e [ə]), it is usually best taught as a short U sound or, better yet for spelling purposes, as a **short E.**

5. **Long A:** The E by itself can sound like a **long A** in foreign names and words derived from foreign words (Jose, bouquet, fiance)

6. **Silent E:** The E is usually **silent** when it is at the end of the word; it serves as a sign that the preceding vowel is long (same, June).

7. **EY:** The EY can sound like a **long E** (key, money, donkey) or like a **long A** (hey, they, survey).

8. **EW:** This pair sounds like **OO** (blew, grew), like a **long U** (few, pew) or like either (new, stew). (See note on page 216.)

9. **ER:** This pair usually sounds like (and is best taught as) the **ER** in HER (baker, perhaps), but it can also sound like **AIR** (berry, sincerity, America) or like **EAR** (cafeteria, period, cereal).

10. **EI:** The EI sometimes sounds like the predicted **long E** (receive, leisure, seize), but it often sounds like a **long A** (beige, weigh, eight) and occasionally like a **long I** (height, seismic).

11. **-LE:** The ending -LE sounds like a **schwa** (short U) **and an L.**

12. **Exceptions:** There are exceptions: been (contradicts item 2), foreign (contradicts item 10), ocean (contradicts item 2), and so on.

This appendix should not be used as a basis for teaching vowels.

CAUTION: As these pages indicate, the sounds for vowels are complex. This section should not be used as a basis for teaching vowels but merely to answer questions that might arise. See page 132 for guidance on teaching vowels.

The Many Voices of I

The vowel sounds are complex and inconsistent.

1. **Short I:** See pages 132, 133, and 208.

2. **Long I:** See pages 132, 133, and 209. The cues for long I are IE (tie, pie) I_E (bite, life), and I at the end of a syllable (i•tem, Fri•day, bi•ceps, di•et).

3. **IE:** This combination can be a **long I,** usually at the end of the word, (die, tie, tried) or it can be a **long E** (believe, brief, niece, field).

4. **IGH:** The IGH has the sound of a **long I** (high, night)—except in EIGH (weigh, neighbor).

5. **IND:** The I in IND is usually a **long I** (find, mind, blind).

6. **ILD:** The I in ILD is usually a **long I** (wild, mild, child).

7. **Other:** The I by itself can sound like a **long E** (radio, piano, kiwi, happiness, India).

8. **Short U or schwa:** The I sometimes sounds like a **short U** (*uh*) in a multi-syllable word (terrible, juvenile). Although this sound is technically a schwa (a brief, unaccented *uh* sound shown in dictionaries as an upside-down e [ə]), it is usually best taught to literacy students as simply a short U sound or, for spelling purposes, as a **short I.**

9. **Silent I:** The I is **silent** in the combination AI (main) and sometimes in the combination EI (ceiling).

10. **IR:** This pair makes the same sound as **ER** (bird, first, firm) but in longer words can sound like **EAR** (irrelevant, irrational).

11. **TION, SION, GION, TIOUS, SIOUS, CIOUS,** and **GIOUS:** The I is silent, but it seems to change the sound of the preceding consonant (nation, occassion, region, cautious, suspicious, religious).

12. **Exceptions:** There are always exceptions: give and since (contradict item 2), height (contradicts the exception in item 4), wind as moving air (contradicts item 5), and so on.

The Many Voices of O

1. **Short O:** See pages 132, 133, and 208.

2. **Long O:** See pages 132, 133, and 209. The cues for long O are OA (boat, oak), OE (toe, doe), O_E (pole, stone), and O at the end of a syllable (o•pen clo•ver, so•fa, so•lo, go).

3. **Other:** Sometimes the O by itself can sound like another vowel:
   • **Short U (accented):** (mother, some, wonder, of, from)
   • **Long O:** (ghost, both, comb, most)
   • **AU:** (off, log, moth)
   • **Long OO:** (to, do, who, tomb)

4. **Short U, unaccented,** or **schwa:** The O may have a schwa sound (see description on previous page) (absolute, button), which can be taught as a **short U** or, for spelling purposes, as a **short O.**

5. **OO:** There are two main sounds for OO: **long OO** (food, boot, tooth) and **short OO** (good, foot, book).

6. **OU:** The OU by itself can sound like **OW** (ouch, south), **short OO** (could, would), **short U** (southern, cousin, young), **long O** (bouquet, soul), or **long OO** (group, youth).

7. **OUS:** The OUS sounds like **US** (famous, anxious). The O is **silent.**

8. **OUGH:** This group can sound like **short U** (rough, enough), **long O** (though, dough), **long OO** (through), or **AU** (bought, cough).

9. **OI** and **OY:** These two pairs have the same sound. OY is generally used on the end of a word (toy) and OI in the middle (toil).

10. **OW:** This can sound like **OU** (cow, town) or like **long O** (own, show).

11. **OLD, OLK, OLL,** and **OLT:** These combinations have the sound of a **long O** (sold, cold, folk, yolk, toll, roll, bolt, colt).

12. **OFT, OSS, OST,** and **ONG:** These groups usually have the sound of **AU** (soft, loft, loss, toss, lost, cost, wrong, song).

13. **OVE:** There are three sounds for OVE: a **long O** (stove, rover), a **short U** (love, shovel, oven), and a **long OO** (move, prove).

14. **OR:** This sounds like **OR** (short, chore) or like **ER** (color, actor).

15. **Exceptions:** There are many exceptions, such as broad (item 2), shoe (item 2), drought (item 8), and women and woman (item 3).

Reminder: This information is for reference only, not for your student to learn.

CAUTION: As these pages indicate, the sounds for vowels are complex. This section should not be used as a basis for teaching vowels but merely to answer questions that might arise. See page 132 for guidance on teaching vowels.

The Many Voices of U

There are two sounds for long U.

1. **Short U:** See pages 132, 133, and 208. (Technically, the U can also be a schwa, a shorter, less stressed version of the short U [circus, spacious], but this knowledge does not help a literacy student.)

2. **Long U:** See pages 132, 133, and 209. The cues for long U are UI, UE, U_E, and a U at the end of a syllable (u•nit, tu•tor, flu).

   Note: **The so-called "long U" is sometimes a true long U (*yoo* as in union, or cue) and sometimes merely an OO (as in true or flu) without the Y sound in front.** Most students do not need to know this. The two sounds are close enough for practical purposes.

3. **UE:** This combination can sound like a **long U** (due, Tuesday, value) or it can be split into two syllables (duet, cruel, fuel), or the pair can be silent at the end of a word (league, fatigue, vague, antique).

4. **Silent U:** A silent U is often found between a G and an I (guide, guitar) or between a G and an E (guess, guest). The U protects the G from the I or E which would make the G soft (see page 127).

5. **UR:** The UR has the same sound as ER and IR (fur, burn, urgent, curl).

6. **UY:** The UY usually has the sound of a **long I** (buy, guy)

7. **ULL:** The ULL has two sounds: a **short U** (dull, gull) and a **short OO** (pull, full).

8. **Exceptions:** There are always exceptions; for example, dunce (contradicts item 2), busy (contradicts item 1) and suite (contradicts item 2).

The Many Voices of Y

1. **At the beginning:** When Y is at the beginning of a word, it usually has a consonant sound (yes, yellow, year).

2. **One-syllable words:** At the end of a one-syllable word, the Y with a consonant before it takes the sound of a **long I** (cry, fly, dry, shy, why).

   However, if the Y is preceded by a vowel, the sound varies with the vowel: day, key, toy, buy.

3. **Multi-syllable words:** In most words of two or more syllables that end with a consonant and a Y, the Y sounds like a **long E**.

baby	lady	memory	suddenly
crazy	berry	fidelity	factory

   Exceptions: rely, defy, deny, July, occupy

4. **IFY:** A notable exception to the above rule is words that end in IFY. The Y sounds like a **long I**.

magnify	clarify	specify	glorify
simplify	beautify	amplify	rectify

5. **In the middle of a word:** When a Y is in the middle of a word, it can be either a consonant, a **short I**, a **long I**, or a **long E**.

consonant	short I	long I	long E
backyard	bicycle	cycle	marrying
lawyer	physical	style	anything
yoyo	oxygen	rhyme	copyright
	gym	flying	
	rhythm	bye	Other
	syllable	type	oyster
		dynamite	payroll
		hyphen	mayor

Basically, the Y serves as either an E or an I.

Appendix E: Beginning and Intermediate Word Families

Beginning

ab	ack	ad	ag	all*	am
cab	back	ad	bag	all	am
dab	hack	add	gag	ball	dam
gab	jack	bad	hag	call	ham
jab	lack	dad	lag	fall	jam
lab	Mack	fad	nag	gall	Pam
nab	pack	had	rag	hall	ram
tab	quack	lad	sag	mall	Sam
	rack	mad	tag	tall	yam
	sack	pad	wag	wall	-------
	tack	sad	-------		sham
	-------	tad	shag		
	shack	-------			
		Chad			

Intermediate

ab	ack	ad	ag	all*	am
blab	black	clad	flag	small	clam
flab	clack	glad	slag	squall	slam
crab	slack	Brad	brag	stall	cram
drab	crack	grad	crag		dram
grab	track		drag		gram
scab	smack		snag		tram
slab	snack		stag		scam
stab	stack		swag		Spam
	whack				swam
	knack				scram

* Although the A in "all" is not short, it is included in the beginner list because of its frequent usage.

an	ap	ar*	ass	ash	at
an	cap	bar	ass	ash	at
Ann	gap	car	bass	bash	bat
ban	lap	far	Cass	cash	cat
can	map	jar	gas	dash	fat
Dan	nap	mar	lass	gash	hat
fan	rap	-------	mass	hash	mat
Jan	sap	char	pass	lash	pat
man	tap		sass	mash	rat
pan	zap			rash	sat
ran	-------			sash	vat
tan	chap				-------
van					chat
-------					that
Chan					
than					

Beginning students who have mastered the words at the top can add the intermediate words at the bottom.

an	ap	ar*	ass	ash	at
clan	clap	scar	class	clash	flat
plan	flap	spar	glass	flash	slat
bran	slap	star	brass	slash	brat
scan	trap		crass	brash	drat
span	snap		grass	crash	frat
Stan	scrap			trash	scat
	strap			smash	spat
	wrap			stash	splat
				splash	gnat
				thrash	
				gnash	

See Strategies 30 and 31 for ideas for using these words.

* Although the A in "ar" is not short, it is included in the beginner list because of its frequent usage.

Beginning

ath	ax	ay*	ee*	eck	ed
bath	ax	bay	be	Beck	Ed
hath	fax	day	bee	deck	bed
math	lax	gay	Dee	heck	fed
path	Max	hay	fee	neck	led
	sax	jay	he	peck	Ned
	tax	lay	Lee	-------	red
	wax	may	me	check	Ted
		pay	see		wed
		ray	tee		
		say	we		
		way	wee		
			ye		
			-------		
			she		

Intermediate words are listed alphabetically in this order:

- L-blends
- R-blends
- S-blends
- other blends

ath	ax	ay*	ee*	eck	ed
wrath	flax	clay	flee	fleck	bled
		play	glee	Breck	fled
		bray	free	speck	pled
		fray	tree	wreck	sled
		gray	spree		Fred
		pray	three		sped
		tray	knee		
		slay			
		stay			
		sway			
		spray			
		stray			

Intermediate

* Although the A in "ay" and the E in "ee" are long, not short, they are included in the beginner list because of their frequent usage and simplicity.

eg	ell	en	ess	et	ex
egg	bell	Ben	Bess	bet	ex
beg	dell	den	less	get	hex
keg	fell	hen	mess	jet	Rex
leg	hell	Ken	yes	let	sex
Meg	jell	men	-------	met	Tex
peg	Nell	pen	chess	net	vex
	quell	ten		pet	-------
	sell	yen		set	Chex
	tell	-------		vet	
	well	then		wet	
	yell			yet	
	-------			-------	
	shell			Chet	

Beginning students who have mastered the words at the top can add the intermediate words at the bottom.

eg	ell	en	ess	et
Greg	cell	Glen	bless	Bret
	gel	wren	dress	fret
	smell	when	press	whet
	spell		stress	
	swell		guess	
	dwell			
	knell			

Beginning

ib	ick	id	ig	ill	im
bib	Dick	bid	big	ill	dim
fib	kick	did	dig	bill	him
lib	lick	hid	fig	dill	Kim
rib	Nick	kid	gig	fill	Jim
	pick	lid	jig	gill	rim
	quick	rid	pig	hill	Tim
	Rick	Sid	rig	Jill	vim
	sick		wig	kill	-------
	tick			mill	shim
	wick			pill	
	-------			quill	
	chick			sill	
	thick			till	
				will	
				-------	
				chill	

Intermediate

ib	ick	id	ig	ill	im
glib	click	slid	brig	drill	slim
crib	flick	grid	sprig	frill	brim
	slick	skid	swig	grill	grim
	brick	squid	twig	trill	prim
	trick			skill	trim
	stick			spill	skim
				still	swim
				shrill	whim
				thrill	

in	ip	iss	ish	it	ix
in	dip	hiss	dish	it	fix
inn	hip	kiss	fish	bit	Kix
bin	lip	miss	wish	fit	mix
din	nip	-------		hit	nix
fin	quip	this		kit	six
kin	rip			lit	
pin	sip			mitt	
sin	tip			pit	
tin	zip			quit	
win	-------			sit	
-------	chip			wit	
chin	ship				
shin					
thin					

in	ip	iss	ish	it
grin	blip	bliss	squish	flit
skin	clip	Swiss	swish	slit
spin	flip			grit
twin	slip			skit
	drip			spit
	grip			split
	trip			twit
	skip			whit
	snip			
	strip			
	whip			

Beginning

o*	ob	ock	od	og(1)	og(2)
go	Bob	cock	odd	-bog	-bog
no	cob	dock	cod	cog	-dog
so	gob	hock	God	-dog	-fog
	job	jock	mod	-fog	-hog
	lob	lock	nod	-hog	-log
	mob	mock	pod	-log	
	rob	pock	rod	jog	
		rock	sod	nog	
		sock	Tod	tog	
		-------	-------		
		chock	shod		
		shock			

Intermediate

o*	ob	ock	od	og(1)	og(2)
bro	blob	block	clod	clog	-flog
fro	slob	clock	plod	-flog	-smog
pro	snob	flock	prod	slog	
	knob	crock	trod	-smog	
		frock	scrod		
		smock			
		stock			
		knock			

Note: OG(1) is a true short O and rhymes with jog, while OG(2) is really AWG and rhymes with the way most Americans say dog. The words marked with a line (-) can be pronounced either way (dictionaries differ). Omit the words that don't match your student's pronunciation, or skip the OG family altogether.

* Although this O is long, not short, it is included in the beginner list because of its simplicity and frequent usage.

Sanilac District Library

on	op	ot	ox	oy*
on	bop	cot	ox	boy
con	cop	dot	box	coy
Don	hop	got	fox	joy
non	mop	hot	pox	Roy
Ron	pop	jot	sox	soy
yon	sop	lot		toy
	top	not		
	-------	pot		
	chop	rot		
	shop	tot		
		-------		
		shot		

op	ot	oy*
clop	blot	ploy
flop	clot	Troy
glop	plot	
plop	slot	
slop	trot	
crop	spot	
drop	knot	
prop		
stop		
whop		

* Although the O in "oy" is not short, it is included in the beginner list because of its frequent usage.

Beginning

ub	uck	ud	uff	ug	um
bub	buck	bud	buff	bug	um
cub	duck	cud	cuff	dug	bum
dub	luck	dud	muff	hug	gum
hub	muck	mud	puff	jug	hum
nub	puck	-------		lug	mum
pub	suck	thud		mug	rum
rub	tuck			pug	sum
sub	yuck			rug	yum
tub	-------			tug	-------
	chuck			-------	chum
	shuck			chug	
				thug	

Intermediate

ub	uck	ud	uff	ug	um
club	cluck	spud	bluff	plug	glum
flub	pluck	stud	fluff	slug	plum
grub	stuck		gruff	drug	drum
snub	struck		scuff	smug	scum
stub	truck		snuff	snug	slum
scrub				shrug	swum
shrub					strum
					-------
					dumb
					numb
					thumb
					plumb
					crumb

un	up	us	ush	ut
bun	up	us	gush	but
fun	cup	bus	hush	butt
gun	pup	cuss	lush	cut
nun	sup	fuss	mush	gut
pun	yup	Gus	rush	hut
run		muss		jut
sun		pus		nut
- - - - - - -				rut
shun				Tut
				- - - - - - -
				shut

un		us	ush	ut
spun		plus	blush	glut
stun			flush	smut
			plush	strut
			brush	
			crush	
			slush	
			thrush	

Appendix F: Intermediate Word Families

Short A

See also Appendix E.

See Strategies 30 and 31 for ideas for using these words.

act	amp	ank	ance	ant	ast
act	amp	bank	dance	ant	cast
fact	camp	dank	lance	can't	fast
pact	damp	hank	chance	pant	last
tact	lamp	lank	France	rant	mast
tract	ramp	rank	glance	chant	past
	tamp	sank	prance	grant	vast
	vamp	tank	stance	plant	blast
	champ	yank	trance	scant	
	clamp	blank		slant	
	cramp	clank			
	stamp	flank			
	tramp	crank			
		drank			
		frank			
		plank			
		prank			
		spank			
		shrank			
		thank			

aft	ang		and	ask	atch
aft	bang		and	ask	batch
raft	fang		band	cask	catch
craft	gang		hand	mask	hatch
draft	hang		land	task	match
graft	pang		sand	flask	scratch
shaft	rang		bland		thatch
	sang		brand		
	tang		gland		
	clang		grand		
	slang		stand		
	sprang		strand		

ace ase

ace	base
face	case
lace	vase
mace	chase
pace	
race	
brace	
grace	
place	
space	
trace	

age

age
cage
page
rage
sage
wage
stage

ake

bake
cake
fake
Jake
lake
make
quake
rake
sake
take
wake
brake
drake
flake
shake
snake
stake

ail ale

ail	ale
bail	bale
fail	dale
Gail	gale
hail	hale
jail	kale
mail	male
nail	pale
pail	sale
quail	tale
rail	vale
sail	Yale
tail	scale
wail	stale
frail	whale
trail	
snail	

aid ade

aid	fade
aide	jade
laid	made
maid	wade
paid	blade
raid	glade
braid	grade
	shade
	spade
	trade

ame

came
dame
fame
game
lame
name
same
tame
blame
flame
frame
shame

aim

aim
maim
claim

Long A

Similar long-vowel families are grouped for comparison.

Long A

ain	ane
gain	cane
lain	Jane
main	lane
pain	mane
rain	pane
vain	sane
brain	vane
chain	wane
drain	plane
grain	crane
plain	
slain	
Spain	
stain	
sprain	
strain	
train	

air	are
air	bare
fair	care
hair	dare
lair	fare
pair	mare
chair	rare
flair	blare
stair	flare
	glare
	scare
	share
	snare
	spare
	square
	stare

ait	ate
bait	ate
gait	date
wait	fate
trait	gate
	hate
	Kate
	late
	mate
	rate
	crate
	grate
	plate
	skate
	slate
	state

ape
ape
cape
gape
nape
rape
tape
grape
scrape
shape

ave
cave
Dave
gave
pave
rave
save
wave
brave
crave
grave
shave
slave

aise	aze
raise	daze
braise	faze
chaise	haze
praise	blaze
	craze

One additional long A family, the AY, is on page 220.

Other Sounds for A

ard
card
guard
hard
lard
yard
chard

arn
barn
darn
yarn

ark
ark
bark
dark
hark
lark
mark
park
Clark
shark
spark
stark

art
art
cart
dart
mart
part
tart
chart
smart
start

arm
arm
farm
harm
charm

arp
carp
harp
tarp
sharp

alk
balk
talk
walk
chalk
stalk

alt
halt
malt
salt

aw
aw
caw
jaw
law
gnaw
paw
raw
saw
claw
craw
draw
flaw
slaw
squaw
straw

aught
caught
naught
taught

aul
haul
maul
Paul

awn
dawn
fawn
lawn
pawn
yawn
drawn
prawn
spawn

awl
awl
bawl
brawl
crawl
drawl
shawl
scrawl
sprawl

Short E

ead	elt	ench	ent	est
(ed)	belt	bench	bent	best
dead	felt	quench	cent	jest
head	melt	wench	dent	lest
(pencil) lead	welt	clench	gent	nest
(past) read	knelt	drench	Kent	pest
bread	smelt	stench	lent	rest
dread		wrench	rent	test
spread			sent	vest
thread			tent	west
tread			vent	zest
			went	blest
		end	scent	chest
			spent	crest
		end		guest
		bend		quest
		fend		
		lend		
		mend		
		rend		
		send	**esh**	
		tend	mesh	
		blend	flesh	
		spend	fresh	
		trend	thresh	

Long E

eal	eel
deal	eel
heal	feel
meal	heel
peal	keel
real	peel
seal	reel
veal	creel
zeal	steel
squeal	wheel
steal	kneel

eam	eem
beam	deem
ream	seem
seam	teem
team	
cream	
dream	
gleam	
scream	
steam	
stream	

ean	een
bean	queen
dean	seen
Jean	teen
lean	sheen
mean	green
wean	screen
clean	
glean	

eak	eek
beak	leek
leak	meek
peak	peek
teak	seek
weak	week
bleak	cheek
creak	creek
sneak	Greek
speak	sleek
squeak	
streak	

eap	eep
heap	deep
leap	jeep
reap	keep
cheap	peep
	seep
	weep
	cheep
	creep
	sheep
	sleep
	steep
	sweep

eat	eet
eat	beet
beat	feet
feat	meet
heat	fleet
meat	greet
neat	sheet
peat	sleet
seat	street
	sweet
	tweet

Long E

e	ee	ea
be	bee	pea
he	Dee	sea
me	fee	tea
we	Lee	flea
ye	see	plea
she	tee	
	wee	
	flee	
	free	
	glee	
	knee	
	spree	
	three	
	tree	

ead (short E)	ead (long E)	eed
dead	bead	deed
head	lead	feed
lead	read	heed
read	plead	need
bread		reed
dread		seed
tread		weed
spread		breed
thread		creed
		freed
		greed
		speed
		steed

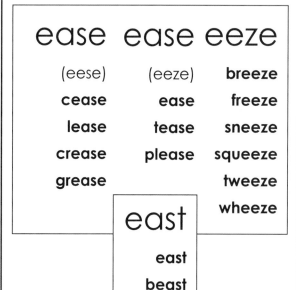

ease (eese)	ease (eeze)	eeze
cease	ease	breeze
lease	tease	freeze
crease	please	sneeze
grease		squeeze
		tweeze
		wheeze

east
east
beast
feast
least
yeast

each	eech
each	beech
beach	leech
leach	breech
peach	screech
reach	speech
teach	
bleach	
breach	
preach	

Other Sounds for E

eigh
(long A)

neigh

weigh

sleigh

eight
(long A)

eight

freight

weight

ey
(long A)

hey

grey

prey

they

whey

er   erve

er	erve
-ber	nerve
-der	serve
-ger	swerve
her	
-ler	
-mer	
-ner	
per	
-ser	
-ter	

ief
(long E)

brief

chief

grief

thief

ew

dew

few

hew

Jew

pew

chew

blew

flew

brew

crew

drew

screw

skew

slew

stew

strew

threw

knew

ear   ear   eer

ear	ear	eer
(air)	ear	beer
bear	dear	deer
wear	fear	jeer
pear	gear	peer
tear	hear	queer
swear	near	sheer
	rear	sneer
	sear	steer
	tear	
	year	
	clear	
	shear	
	smear	
	spear	

Short I

iff	ift	ilt	isk	ing	ink
if	gift	built	disk	ding	ink
cliff	lift	guilt	risk	king	kink
skiff	rift	jilt	brisk	ping	link
sniff	drift	kilt	frisk	ring	mink
stiff	shift	quilt	whisk	sing	pink
	swift	silt		wing	rink
	thrift	tilt		zing	sink
		wilt		bring	wink
		spilt		cling	blink
		stilt		fling	brink
				sling	chink
				spring	drink
				sting	shrink
				string	stink
				swing	
				thing	
				wring	

itch	inch	ince	int	ist
itch	inch	mince	hint	list
bitch	cinch	since	lint	mist
ditch	finch	wince	mint	wrist
pitch	pinch	prince	tint	grist
witch	winch		flint	twist
glitch	clinch		glint	
snitch	flinch		print	
stitch			splint	
switch			sprint	
			squint	
			stint	

Long I

y	ye	ie	igh
by	bye	die	high
my	dye	fie	nigh
cry	lye	lie	sigh
dry	rye	pie	thigh
fly		tie	
fry		vie	
ply			
pry			
shy			
sky			
sly			
spry			
spy			
sty			
thy			
try			
why			

ight	ite
fight	bite
light	kite
might	mite
night	quite
right	rite
sight	site
tight	spite
blight	sprite
bright	white
flight	write
fright	
knight	
plight	
slight	

ile	ime
bile	dime
file	lime
mile	mime
Nile	time
pile	chime
tile	clime
vile	crime
smile	grime
while	prime
	slime

ibe	ife	ike
jibe	fife	bike
bribe	life	dike
tribe	wife	hike
scribe	knife	like
	strife	Mike
		pike
		spike
		strike

Long I and IR

ine	ice	ise	ide	ipe	ive
dine	(ise)	(ize)	bide	pipe	dive
fine	ice	rise	hide	ripe	five
line	dice	wise	ride	wipe	hive
mine	lice	guise	side	gripe	jive
nine	mice		tide	snipe	live
pine	nice		wide	swipe	chive
tine	rice		bride	stripe	drive
vine	vice		chide	tripe	strive
wine	price		glide		thrive
brine	slice		pride		
shine	spice		slide		
shrine	splice		snide		
spine	thrice		stride		
swine	twice				
whine					

ild	ind	ire	irt	irl
mild	bind	ire	dirt	girl
wild	find	fire	flirt	swirl
child	hind	hire	shirt	twirl
	kind	tire	skirt	whirl
	mind	wire	squirt	
	rind	spire		
	wind	squire		
	blind			
	grind			

Short O and------------Long O

ond

bond
fond
pond
blond
frond

obe

lobe
robe
globe
probe
strobe

oach

coach
poach
roach

oad ode

oad	ode
load	ode
road	code
toad	lode
	mode
	node
	rode

otch

botch
notch
blotch
crotch
Scotch

oak oke

oak	oke
oak	coke
soak	joke
cloak	poke
croak	woke
	broke
	choke
	smoke
	spoke
	stoke
	stroke

oam ome

oam	ome
foam	dome
loam	home
roam	Rome
	tome
	gnome
	chrome

Similar families are grouped for comparison.

on

on
con
Don
Ron

om

Tom
mom
pom-pom

oal ole oll

oal	ole	oll
coal	dole	poll
foal	hole	roll
goal	mole	toll
shoal	pole	scroll
	role	stroll
	stole	troll
	whole	

old olt

old	olt
old	bolt
bold	colt
cold	jolt
fold	molt
gold	volt
hold	
mold	
sold	
told	
scold	

Long O

oan one

Joan	bone
loan	cone
moan	hone
groan	lone
	tone
	zone
	clone
	crone
	drone
	phone
	prone
	stone

ope

cope
dope
hope
lope
mope
nope
pope
rope
grope
scope
slope

oe   ōw   ow

oe	ōw	ow
doe	low	(ou)
foe	bow	ow
hoe	mow	cow
Joe	row	how
toe	sow	bow
woe	tow	now
	blow	sow
	crow	vow
	flow	brow
	glow	chow
	grow	plow
	know	
	show	
	slow	
	snow	
	stow	
	throw	

ose

hose
nose
pose
rose
chose
close
prose
those

oast   ōst   ost

oast	ōst	ost
boast	host	(au)
coast	most	cost
roast	post	lost
toast	ghost	frost

ōve   ove

ōve	ove
cove	(uv)
dove	dove
wove	love
clove	glove
drove	shove
grove	
stove	

oat   ote

oat	ote
oat	note
boat	quote
coat	rote
goat	vote
moat	wrote
bloat	
float	
throat	

241

Other Sounds for O

oy	oar	ore	orn	ought
boy	boar	ore	born	bought
coy	roar	bore	corn	fought
joy	soar	core	horn	ought
Roy		fore	morn	sought
soy		gore	torn	brought
toy		more	worn	thought
ploy		pore	scorn	
Troy		sore	shorn	**oss**
		tore	sworn	boss
		wore	thorn	loss
oil		chore		moss
		score		toss
oil		shore		cross
boil		store		floss
coil		swore		gloss
foil				
soil				
toil	**orch**	**ork**	**ort**	**ong**
broil				
spoil	porch	cork	fort	bong
	torch	fork	Mort	gong
	scorch	York	port	long
oin		stork	sort	song
			short	tong
coin	**ord**		snort	prong
join			sport	strong
loin	cord		tort	thong
groin	Ford			wrong
	lord			throng
	sword			

Other Sounds: $\overline{oo}$ and $\breve{oo}$

$\overline{oo}$	$\breve{oo}k$	$\overline{oo}l$	$\overline{oo}m$	$\overline{oo}p$	$\overline{oo}t$
coo	book	cool	boom	hoop	boot
goo	cook	fool	doom	loop	hoot
moo	hook	pool	loom	droop	loot
too	look	drool	room	scoop	moot
woo	took	school	bloom	sloop	root
zoo	brook	spool	broom	snoop	toot
shoo	crook	stool	gloom	swoop	scoot
	shook		groom	troop	shoot

ould	$\breve{oo}d$	$\overline{oo}d$	$\overline{oo}n$	$\overline{oo}se$
could	good	food	boon	goose
would	hood	mood	loon	loose
should	wood	brood	moon	moose
	stood		noon	noose
			soon	
			croon	
			spoon	
			swoon	

OU/OW---and Other Sounds for O

owl	ouch	ouse	ough
owl	ouch	douse	rough
fowl	couch	house	tough
howl	pouch	louse	enough
jowl	crouch	mouse	
growl	grouch	souse	
prowl	slouch	grouse	
scowl		spouse	

own	ōwn	ounce	out	other
(oun)	own	ounce	out	other
down	blown	bounce	bout	mother
gown	flown	pounce	pout	brother
town	grown	flounce	grout	smother
brown	known	trounce	scout	
clown	shown		shout	
crown			spout	
drown		ound	sprout	
frown			stout	
		bound	trout	
		found		
		hound		
		mound		
		pound		
		round		
		sound		
		ground		

Short U

udge	ump	ung	unk	ull
fudge	ump	hung	bunk	dull
judge	bump	lung	dunk	gull
nudge	dump	rung	funk	hull
grudge	hump	sung	hunk	lull
sludge	jump	clung	junk	mull
	lump	flung	punk	skull
	pump	slung	sunk	
	rump	sprung	chunk	
	sump	stung	drunk	
	chump	strung	flunk	
	clump	swung	plunk	
	frump	wrung	shrunk	
	grump		skunk	
	plump		slunk	
	slump		spunk	
	stump		stunk	
	trump		trunk	

umb	unch	unt	ust	utch
dumb	bunch	bunt	bust	Dutch
numb	hunch	hunt	dust	hutch
crumb	lunch	punt	just	clutch
plumb	munch	runt	lust	crutch
thumb	punch	blunt	rust	
	brunch	grunt	thrust	
	crunch	stunt	trust	

Long U and UR

ue	ube	ude	uke	une	ute
due	cube	dude	cuke	June	jute
hue	lube	nude	duke	tune	lute
sue	tube	rude	Luke	prune	flute
blue		crude	fluke		brute
clue		prude			
flue					
glue					

ur	urge	url	urn	urse	urt
burr	urge	curl	urn	curse	curt
fur	purge	furl	burn	nurse	hurt
purr	surge	hurl	turn	purse	blurt
blur	splurge		churn		spurt
slur			spurn		
spur					

Appendix G: Compound Words

A

afternoon
aftershave
aftertaste
airbag
airline
airplane
airport
airsick
airtight
anybody
anyhow
anymore
anyone
anyplace
anything
anytime
anyway
anywhere
armchair
armhole
armpit
armrest

B

backache
backbone
background
backpack
ballroom
bankbook
barbell
barefoot
barnyard
barroom
bartender
baseball
basketball
bathrobe

bathroom
bathtub
bedpan
bedroom
bedspread
bedtime
become
bellhop
beside
birdbath
birdhouse
birdseed
birthday
blackberry
blackboard
blackmail
blackout
blacktop
blindfold
blowout
blueberry
bookcase
bookends
bookkeeper
bookmark
bookshelf
boxcar
bridesmaid
broadcast
Broadway
butterfly
buttermilk
butternut

C

candlelight
candlestick
cardboard
carload
carpool
carsick

catfish
cattail
catwalk
checkbook
checkroom
cheeseburger
cheesecake
chopsticks
clubhouse
cowboy
crossbar
crossroad
crosswalk
crossword
crybaby
cupcake
cutback

D

daylight
daytime
deadline
deadlock
dogcatcher
dogfight
doghouse
downstairs
downtown
drawback
drawstring
drugstore
drumbeat
drumstick
dustpan

E

earache
eardrum
earlobe

earmuff
earphone
earplug
earring
earshot
earwax
earthquake
earthworm
evergreen
everlasting
everybody
everyone
everything
everywhere
eyeball
eyedropper
eyelash
eyelid
eyesight

F

farmhand
farmhouse
farmland
farmyard
fingernail
fingerprint
firefighter
fireplace
fireplug
fireproof
firewood
fireworks
fishbowl
fishhook
flagpole
flashlight
floodlight
flowerpot
foghorn
foolproof

See Strategy 44 for ideas for using these words.

football
footlights
footnote
footpath
footprint
footstep
footstool
forearm
forecast
forefinger
foreground
forehead
forever
forklift
foxhole
freeway
freshwater
frostbite
fruitcake
fullback

G

gearshift
gentleman
goalkeeper
goalpost
goddaughter
godfather
godmother
godson
goldfish
goodwill
gooseberry
grandchild
grandchildren
granddaughter
grandfather
grandmother
grandparent
grandson
grandstand

grapefruit
grapevine
gravestone
graveyard
greenhouse
Greenland
grownup
guardhouse
guardrail
gunfire
gunshot

H

hairbrush
haircut
hairdo
hairdresser
halfback
hallway
handbag
handmade
handout
handsaw
handshake
handstand
hangout
hangover
hardware
hardwood
headache
headboard
headlight
headphone
headquarters
headrest
headroom
hemline
herself
highlight
highway
hillside

hilltop
himself
homecoming
homemade
homemaker
homeroom
homesick
homework
horseback
horsefly
horsepower
horseradish
horseshoe
hotshot
houseboat
housebroken
houseclean
housefly
household
housetop
housework
however
hubcap

I

icebox
Iceland
inchworm
income
infield
inside
into
itself

K

kickback
kickstand
kidnap
kneecap

L

ladybug
lakeside
landlady
landlord
landmark
landslide
lawsuit
leftovers
lifeboat
lifeguard
lifesaver
lifetime
lighthouse
lineup
lipstick
lookout
loophole
loudmouth
loudspeaker
lovebirds
lovesick
lowdown
lunchroom

M

madhouse
mailbox
manhunt
manpower
mealtime
meantime
meatball
midnight
milestone
moonlight
mousetrap
mouthwash
myself

248

N

neckline
necktie
newscast
newsletter
newspaper
newsstand
nightclub
nightfall
nightgown
nightlife
nighttime
nobody
northeast
northwest
notebook
nowhere
nutcracker
nutshell

O

oatmeal
oddball
offside
offspring
oncoming
ongoing
otherwise
outcast
outcome
outdated
outdoors
outfield
outfit
outlaw
outlet
outline
output
outrage

outreach
outside
overcoat
overcome
overdrive
overflow
overhang
overhead
overhear
overlook
overnight
overpass
overpay
oversee
oversleep
overstep
overtake
overthrow
overturn
overview

P

pancake
paperback
Passover
passport
password
pathway
pawnshop
paycheck
payday
payroll
peacemaker
peacetime
peanut
pickpocket
pickup
piggyback
pigpen
pineapple
pinhole

pinpoint
pipeline
playback
playground
playhouse
playmate
playpen
playsuit
plaything
popcorn
postcard
postmark
pothole
potluck
printout

Q

quarterback
quicksand

R

railroad
rainbow
raincoat
raindrop
rainfall
rainwater
rattlesnake
redhead
restroom
riverbank
riverboat
riverside
roadblock
roadside
roadway
roadwork
roommate
rosebud

rosebush
runway

S

sailboat
salesperson
saltwater
sandbag
sandbar
sandbox
sandpaper
sandstorm
sawdust
sawhorse
sawmill
schoolboy
schoolgirl
schoolhouse
schoolteacher
scrapbook
seacoast
seafood
seahorse
seaport
seashore
seasick
seaside
seawater
seaweed
sheepskin
shipyard
shoelace
shoestring
shoplift
shortcake
shortcoming
shortcut
shortstop
showcase
showdown
shutdown

shutout
sideburns
sideshow
sidewalk
sideways
silverware
skylight
skyline
skyscraper
slowpoke
snapshot
snowball
snowdrift
snowflake
snowman
snowplow
snowshoe
snowstorm
softball
software
softwood
somebody
someday
somehow
someone
something
sometime
somewhere
southeast
southwest
spotlight
springtime
staircase
stairway
starfish
starlight
steamboat
steamship
stepbrother
stepchild
stepdaughter
stepfather
stepladder

stepmother
stepsister
stepson
stoplight
stopwatch
storehouse
storeroom
strawberry
streetcar
suitcase
summertime
sunburn
sundown
sunglasses
sunlamp
sunlight
sunrise
sunset
sunshine
sunstroke
suntan
sweetheart

T

tablecloth
tablespoon
tailgate
taillight
teacup
teakettle
teamwork
teapot
teaspoon
textbook
Thanksgiving
thumbnail
thumbtack
thundershower
thunderstorm
tiptoe
tollgate

tomcat
toothache
toothbrush
toothpaste
toothpick
topcoat
topsoil
touchdown
trademark
tugboat
turnpike

U

undercover
underdog
underdone
underground
underhand
underline
underpass
understand
underwear
uphill
uplift
upright
upset
upstairs
uptight
uptown

W

waistband
waistline
wallpaper
wartime
washcloth
wastebasket
wastepaper
watchband

watchdog
waterbed
waterfall
waterproof
watertight
weekday
weekend
whatever
wheelbarrow
wheelchair
whichever
whiplash
whoever
wholesale
windproof
windshield
wintertime
wisecrack
wishbone
within
without
woodpile
woodshed
woodwork
workbasket
workbench
workbook
workday
workout
workroom
workshop
worldwide
worthwhile
wristband
wristwatch

Y

yardstick
yearbook
yearlong
yourself

Appendix H:
Long Words

H1 *Two-Consonant Rule*
First Practice Set

This list contains two-syllable words that are basically phonetic and have two consonants in the middle. Advanced students can practice these words using Strategy 45.

abduct	barber	burden	chipmunk
absent	barley	burger	cluster
actor	basket	butter	clutter
addict	batter	cactus	cobweb
album	better	campus	coffin
amber	blubber	carpet	collect
ambush	Bombay	carton	combat
annoy	border	catfish*	command
attic	bottom	channel	common
bandit	boxcar*	chapter	compact
banner	bucket	chatter	conduct
Baptist	bumper	chimney	confirm

* The Two-Consonant Rule can also be used on words that are not first recognized as compound words. A few examples are included above.

See Strategy 45 for ideas for using these words.

THE TWO-CONSONANT RULE

If there are two consonants between the vowels, cut the word between the consonants.

in|to   les|son   traf|fic   fen|der

Two-Consonant Rule: First Practice Set

consent	enroll	furnish	husband
contest	enter	garden	index
convict	expand	garment	inform
copper	expect	garter	inject
corner	expert	goblin	inning
cornet	export	golden	insect
correct	fabric	gossip	insert
current	farmer*	gotten	insist
Denmark	fellow	hammer	insult
dentist	fender	happen	invent
Denver	filter	hello	jacket
dessert	Finland	helmet	Kansas
discuss	foghorn*	hermit	kidney
disgust	follow	hiccup	kitten
dismiss	forget	Holland	ladder
doctor	forgot	hollow	lantern
elbow	former	hubbub	lesson
enlist*	fragment	hubcap*	letter

* The Two-Consonant Rule can also be used on words that the student does not recognize as compound words or as words with a prefix suffix. A few examples are included above.

Two-Consonant Rule: First Practice Set

litter	napkin	plaster	reddish
locket	network	plastic	ribbon
lumber	nitwit	platform	robber
madness*	number	pocket	rocker
magnet	nutmeg	popcorn*	rocket
manner	object	porter	rubber
market	offer	possum	sadness*
mascot	orbit	potluck*	sandal
master	order	powder	scandal
member	packet	powwow	scatter
mental	pardon	pregnant	Scotland
midnight	pattern	pretzel	segment
misfit	pepper	printer*	seldom
mitten	perfect	problem	serpent
morning	perform	public	shelter
muffin	person	publish	shipment
mustang	picnic	puppet	silver
mustard	pillow	rabbit	simmer
mutter	piston	ragged	sister

* The Two-Consonant Rule will also work for words that the student does not recognize as compound words or as words with a suffix.

Two-Consonant Rule: First Practice Set

skillet	suspect	unlock*	warden**
slender	suspend	unpack*	wedding*
slippers	target	until	wedlock
sluggish	temper	unzip*	western
slumber	tennis	uplift*	whimper
spatter	thunder	upper	whisper
splatter	tractor	upset*	wicker
splendid	traffic	varnish	wigwam**
splinter*	trespass	velvet	willow
starfish*	triplets	verdict	window
stoplight*	trumpet	Vermont	winter
sudden	tunnel	vessel	wisdom
suffer	twister	victim	witness
summer	under	wallet**	yellow
sunburn*	unfit*	walrus**	yonder
supper	unfold*	walnut**	zigzag
support	unless	wander**	zipper*

* The Two-Consonant Rule will also work for words that the student does not recognize as compound words or as words with a prefix or suffix.

** The A in a WA- combination often sounds like AU, AH, or OR, or rather than short A (as in wax).

H2

Two-Consonant Rule
Second Practice Set

This set of words can be used for practice as part of Strategy 46, harder versions of the Two-Consonant Rule.

These words are more difficult than words in the preceding list because they contain such complications as:

- Silent E's on the end (cross them off).
- Y's on the end. Most sound like long E's but some sound like long I's.
- Double vowels (OO, OY, OW).
- The special endings -TION (shun), -SION (shun), or -TURE (chur).
- Soft C's (sound like S) or soft G's (sound like J).
- Three or more syllables.

accent	attendance	canteen
acquit	attendant	capture
action	attention	carpenter
admission	badger	cartoon
advance	baggy	center
advantage	belly	chimpanzee
advertise	booklet	citrus
advice	buddy	coffee
advise	cabbage	collide
affection	cancel	combine
antenna	cancer	committee
appendix	candy	commute

See Strategy 46 for suggestions on using these words.

Two-Consonant Rule: Second Practice Set

compete	estate	immune
compute	excellent	important
concern	except	infection
concert	excuse	informal
confine	fancy	inquire
confirm	fantastic	interfere
convince	fiction	invade
costume	fifteen	invite
council	fixture	jelly
curfew	forgave	Kentucky
dirty	forgive	lawyer
discount	forgetful	lobby
dusty	forgotten	maintain
embargo	fraction	mansion
enjoy	friction	mention
entertain	funny	messenger
entire	gender	midwife
envy	hamburger	mistake
escape	hobby	mixture
establish	ignore	nasty

Two-Consonant Rule: Second Practice Set

Norway	raccoon	thirteen
office	really	trespassing
parcel	reptile	trombone
party	section	turkey
passenger	session	turpentine
pasture	shabby	twenty
pencil	shampoo	ugly
pension	silly	ulcer
percussion	silverware	umpire
perfect	sissy	unhappy
performance	sturdy	warranty
perfume	success	welcome
personnel	suddenly	welfare
picture	suggest	whiskey
plenty	suggestion	wilderness
practice	suppose	windy
pretty	surrender	Wisconsin
princess	tadpole	witty
puppy	tardy	written
question	Tennessee	yesterday

H3

One-Consonant Rule
First Practice Set

Advanced students can practice these words using Strategy 47.

agent	decoy	evil	humid
baby	defend	fatal	humor
bacon	demand	favor	Irish
bagel	demon	female	item
began	deny	fever	joker
begun	depart	fiber	July
bison	depend	final	label
bonus	donate	flavor	labor
broken	duty	focus	lady
china	elect	Friday	later
crater	elope	frozen	lazy
crazy	equal	gravy	local
crisis	erase	halo	major
Cuba	even	holy	meter
decay	event	hotel	minor
decide	evict	human	molar

THE ONE-CONSONANT RULE

If there is only one consonant between the vowels, divide the word before the consonant and make the first vowel long.

ē|ven   sō|ber   prē|tend   shā|ky

See Strategy 47 for suggestions on using these words.

One-Consonant Rule: First Practice Set

moment	pretend	repair	station
motel	prevent	repeat	stolen
motion	proceed	report	student
motor	produce	require	super
music	promote	retail	taken
navy	propose	retire	tidy
odor	protect	return	tiger
okay	protest	robot	tiny
open	provide	ruby	token
over	pupil	shady	total
ozone	radar	shaken	truly
paper	razor	shaky	tuna
photo	recess	shiny	tutor
pilot	reduce	silent	vacant
poker	refill	siren	veto
Poland	reform	sober	virus
polite	refund	soda	wavy
pony	refuse	sofa	woven
prefer	relax	solo	yoga
preheat	remain	spider	yogurt
preset	remark	spoken	zero

H4

Combination: Two- and One-Consonant Rules

This practice set combines the Two-Consonant and One-Consonant Rules with complications described on page 162. Refer to Strategies 45-48.

NOTE: In longer words, vowel sounds are sometimes softened or distorted in normal speech. We often say coh-cuh-nut, not coh-coh-nut, and uh-lec-tion, not ee-lec-tion. However, it can be beneficial to pronounce the words with exaggerated vowel sounds (coh-coh-nut and ee-lec-tion) when studying. This will help the student learn to spell the words.

absolute	donation	November	relation
adjacent	education	observation	remember
agency	election	occupation	republic
argument	emergency	occupy	romantic
beginning	equipment	occurrence	rotation
carnation	eruption	October	sensation
cloverleaf	eternal	paperback	spectator
coconut	eviction	pollution	supervision
computer	flotation	porcupine	supervisor
conversation	independent	potato	tomato
cucumber	information	prediction	tornado
December	innocent	production	united
defendant	invasion	profession	vacancy
dependent	location	protection	vacation
diploma	locomotion	rejection	volcano

See Strategy 48 for suggestions on using these words.

H5

One-Consonant — Oops Rule
First Practice Set

This list contains two-syllable words that are basically phonetic and follow the One-Consonant — Oops Rule. Advanced students can practice these words using Strategy 49.

baboon	clever	divide	govern
banish	closet	divorce	gravel
body	colic	dragon	habit
bowel	comet	driven	honey
boxer	comics	during	Japan
British	copy	edit	jewel
cabin	coral	ever	Jewish
camel	cover	exact	jury
cavern	credit	exam	Latin
chapel	critic	exist	lemon
city	denim	exit	level
civic	devil	gavel	lever
civil	digit	given	lily

See Strategies 45-49 for suggestions on using these words.

THE ONE-CONSONANT — OOPS RULE

Sometimes the One-Consonant Rule does not work. When that happens, divide the word after the consonant. The vowel is short.

lem/on   vis/it   sec/ond   ov/en   trav/el

One-Consonant—Rule: First Practice Set

limit	oven	robin	tenant
linen	panel	salad	topic
liver	panic	satin	tower
lizard	pedal	Saturn	toxic
loyal	petal	second	trapeze
madam	phonics	secure	travel
magic	pity	sedan	tribute
manor	planet	seven	tropics
medal	polish	sever	valid
medic	power	severe	value
melon	product	sexy	vanish
menu	profit	shadow	vigor
metal	proper	shiver	visit
model	proverb	shovel	volume
modern	punish	sliver	vomit
modest	radish	solid	vowel
money	rapid	Spanish	wagon
moral	rebel	study	waxy
never	relish	suburb	widow
novel	river	tavern	wizard

H6

All Three Rules
Final Practice Set

This list contains multi-syllable words that are basically phonetic and can be divided using a combination of the three rules on page 167.

activate	different	medical	referee
agriculture	discover	minister	regular
aspirin	eleven	narcotics	regulations
balcony	energy	operate	relaxation
beverage	envelope	operator	reverent
cabinet	evolution	operation	salary
calendar	family	opportunity	satellite
caterpillar	Germany	permanent	satisfaction
celery	government	popular	Saturday
company	governor	population	semester
continent	Hispanic	poverty	separate
continue	history	preparation	several
decorate	lavender	president	tranquilizer
deliver	liberty	promise	vanilla
develop	magnetic	recognize	volunteer

See Strategies 45-49 for ideas for using these words.

Appendix J: Contractions

A contraction is a word formed by combining two words and taking out one or more letters. An apostrophe shows where the letters have been removed.

is + not = isnot = isn't   **we + have = wehave = we've**

The examples below show the two-word pair followed by its contraction. Note that some contractions are the same: "It is" and "it has" both contract to the form "it's."

am

I am .... I'm

are

we are ...... we're
you are ..... you're
they are .... they're

is

he is .... he's
she is .... she's
it is .... it's
what is ..... what's
that is .... that's
who is ...... who's
there is ..... there's
here is ...... here's

us

let us .... let's

not

is not .... isn't
are not .... aren't
was not .... wasn't
were not ..... weren't
has not .... hasn't
have not ..... haven't
had not .... hadn't
do not .... don't*
does not ..... doesn't
did not .... didn't
will not .... won't*
can not .... can't
could not ..... couldn't
should not ... shouldn't
would not ... wouldn't

will

I will .... I'll
you will ...... you'll
she will ...... she'll
he will .... he'll
it will .... it'll
we will .... we'll
they will ..... they'll

have

I have .... I've
you have .... you've
we have .... we've
they have ...... they've

has

he has .... he's
she has .... she's
it has .... it's
who has .... who's

had (same as would)

I had .... I'd
you had .... you'd
she had .... she'd
he had .... he'd
we had .... we'd
they had .... they'd

would (same as had)

I would .... I'd
you would ..... you'd
she would ..... she'd
he would .... he'd
we would ...... we'd
they would .... they'd

A contraction is a word formed by combining two words and taking out one or more letters.

See Strategy 12 for suggestions on using these words (even if your student is not ESL).

*The pronunciation of "won't" and "don't" change in the contracted form.

Appendix K:
Sight Words

Beginning Sight Word List

a	have	said	was
all	his	some	water
are	is	the	were
as	Mr.	there	what
come	Mrs.	they	who
do	of	this	woman
does	old	to	women
from	on	two	words
give	one	very	work
has	put	want	you

Intermediate Sight Word List

again	could	knew	school
against	country	know	shoe
answer	danger	laugh	should
any	done	learn	somebody
anybody	double	listen	sorry
anywhere	early	live	such
aunt	eight	love	sure
beautiful	enough	many	their
beauty	eyes	most	thought
become	father	mother	through
been	few	move	touch
both	find	Ms.	uncle
build	four	much	view
business	friends	nothing	war
busy	gone	often	watch
buy	great	once	where
Christmas	group	only	which
city	heard	other	whole
color	hour	people	whose
comb	kind	says	world

See Strategy 33 for suggestions on using these words.

Advanced Sight Word List

ache	earth	mountain	steak
aisle	error	natural	stomach
although	example	nobody	straight
among	February	ocean	strength
ancient	foreign	orange	sure
angel	front	ought	sword
area	ghost	physical	thorough
avenue	golf	physician	though
bicycle	great	picture	tongue
bouquet	half	piece	tough
break	height	plaid	toward
breakfast	honest	prove	trouble
choir	hymn	rhyme	truth
climb	iron	rhythm	Tuesday
clothes	island	rough	usual
colonel	juice	scene	usually
cough	length	sew	vague
cousin	liquor	soldier	Wednesday
debt	measure	soul	yacht
door	minute	sponge	young

Five of the Hardest Words to Learn

tough	(tuff)	This meat is **tough**.
though	(tho)	He was late even **though** he started early.
thought	(thawt)	He **thought** he was on time.
through	(thru)	Are you **through** with the machine?
thorough	(ther-row)	She did a **thorough** job.

Appendix L:
Common Signs

10 ITEMS OR FEWER (LESS)
ADULTS ONLY
ALL SALES FINAL
BEWARE
BEWARE OF DOG
BUS STOP
CASH ONLY
CAUTION
CHECKS CASHED HERE
CHILDREN MUST BE
    ACCOMPANIED BY ADULT
CLOSED
COMBUSTIBLE
CONDEMNED
COUPON

DANGER
DEEP WATER
DENTIST
DEPOSIT 2 QUARTERS
DO NOT CROSS
DO NOT ENTER
DO NOT FLUSH
DO NOT INHALE FUMES
DO NOT PUSH
DO NOT REFREEZE
DO NOT TAKE INTERNALLY
DO NOT TOUCH
DO NOT USE
DO NOT USE AFTER (DATE)
DO NOT USE NEAR HEAT
DO NOT USE NEAR OPEN FLAME
DOCTOR (DR.)
DON'T WALK
DOWN

ELEVATOR
EMERGENCY EXIT
EMERGENCY USE ONLY

EMPLOYEES ONLY
ENTRANCE
EXACT CHANGE ONLY
EXIT
EXIT ONLY
EXPIRES (DATE)
EXPLOSIVES
EXTERNAL USE ONLY
FIRE ESCAPE
FIRE EXTINGUISHER
FIRST AID
FLAMMABLE
FOUND
FRAGILE
FREE

GAS
GENTLEMEN
HANDLE WITH CARE
HANDS OFF
HELP
HELP WANTED
HIGH VOLTAGE
HOSPITAL
IN
IN CASE OF FIRE,
    BREAK GLASS
INFLAMMABLE
INFORMATION
INSERT COIN
INSTRUCTIONS

KEEP AWAY
KEEP CLOSED AT ALL TIMES
KEEP DOOR CLOSED
KEEP OFF (THE GRASS)
KEEP OUT
KEEP PETS ON LEASH
KNOCK BEFORE ENTERING

See Strategy 33 for suggestions on using these words.

LADIES
LAUNDROMAT
LIVE WIRES
LOST (AND FOUND)
MEN
MINORS PROHIBITED
MOVED

NEXT GATE PLEASE
NEXT WINDOW
NO ADMITTANCE
NO ALCOHOLIC BEVERAGES
NO CHECKS
NO DIVING
NO DOGS ALLOWED
NO DUMPING
NO FIRES
NO FISHING
NO LOITERING
NO MINORS
NO RETURNS
NO SMOKING
NO STANDING
NO SWIMMING
NO TRESPASSING
NON-SMOKING AREA
NOT FOR INTERNAL USE
NOW HIRING

OFFICE
OFFICE HOURS
OPEN
OUT
OUT OF ORDER
PLAYGROUND
PLEASE BE SEATED
PLEASE KNOCK
PLEASE WAIT
POISON

POISONOUS
POLICE (STATION)
POST NO BILLS
POST OFFICE
PRIVATE
PRIVATE PROPERTY
PULL
PUSH

RESTAURANT
RESTROOMS
RETURNS
SALE
SCHOOL
SHAKE WELL BEFORE USING
SHALLOW WATER
SHELTER
SHOPLIFTERS WILL BE
     PROSECUTED
SMOKING PROHIBITED
STAY BEHIND YELLOW LINE
STEP DOWN
STEP UP

THIN ICE
THIS END UP
THIS SIDE UP
TICKETS
UP
USE BEFORE (DATE)
VIOLATORS WILL BE
          PROSECUTED
WAIT HERE FOR NEXT TELLER
WALK
WANTED
WARNING
WATCH YOUR STEP
WET PAINT
WOMEN

Appendix M:
Driving Survival Words

AIR
ALL CARS STOP
ALL TRUCKS STOP
AMBULANCE
ASK ATTENDANT FOR KEY

BEWARE OF CROSS WINDS
BRIDGE OUT
BUCKLE UP
BUSES ONLY

CASH
CAUTION
CONSTRUCTION ZONE
CREDIT CARD
CURVE

DANGER
DEAD END
DETOUR
DIM LIGHTS
DIP
DO NOT BLOCK DRIVE
DO NOT ENTER
DO NOT PASS
DRIFTING SAND
DRIFTING SNOW
DRIVE THRU

EMERGENCY VEHICLES ONLY
END 45
END CONSTRUCTION
ENTRANCE
EXIT ONLY
EXIT SPEED 30

FALLING ROCKS
FERRY
FOOD

FOUR WAY STOP
FREEWAY ENDS
FULL SERVE

GAS
GASOLINE
GATES
GO SLOW

HANDICAPPED PARKING
HIDDEN DRIVE
HOSPITAL
HOTEL
INSPECTION STATION
JUNCTION 101
KEEP LEFT
KEEP RIGHT EXCEPT TO PASS

LANE ENDS
LAST CHANCE FOR GAS
LEFT
LIGHTS ON
LOADING ZONE
LOAD LIMIT 10 TONS
LODGING
MERGE
MOTEL

NEXT LEFT
NEXT RIGHT
NEXT EXIT 20 MILES
NO PARKING
NO PARKING HERE TO CORNER
NO PASSING
NO RIGHT TURN ON RED
NO STANDING
NO STOPPING
NO THRU TRAFFIC
NO TRUCKS

See Strategy 33 for suggestions on using these words.

NO TURNS
NO U TURN
NO VACANCY
NO WINTER MAINTENANCE
NOT A THRU STREET

OIL
ONE LANE BRIDGE
ONE WAY— DO NOT ENTER
ONE WAY STREET
ONLY

PARK
PARKING
PATROLLED BY RADAR
PAVEMENT ENDS
PAY ATTENDANT
PAY TOLL AHEAD
PED XING
POLICE
PREPARE TO STOP
PRIVATE DRIVE
PROCEED WITH CAUTION

R.R.
RR XING
RAILROAD CROSSING
REDUCE SPEED
RESUME SPEED
REST AREA
REST STOP
RESTAURANT
RESTROOMS
RIGHT
ROAD CLOSED
ROAD ENDS
ROAD WORK AHEAD
ROADSIDE STOP
ROUGH PAVEMENT

SCENIC DRIVE
SCENIC OVERLOOK
SCHOOL
SELF SERVE
SLIPPERY WHEN WET
SLOW
SLOWER TRAFFIC KEEP RIGHT
SOFT SHOULDER
SOUND HORN
SPEED CHECKED BY RADAR
STEEP GRADE
STOP
STOP AHEAD
STOP AT GATE
STOP FOR PEDESTRIANS
STOP MOTOR
STOP WHEN BUS STOPS

TAXI STAND
THREE WAY STOP
THRU
TRAFFIC CIRCLE
TRUCK ROUTE
TRUCKS PROHIBITED
TRUCKS USE LOW GEAR
TUNNEL
TURN OFF ENGINE

USE LOW GEAR
VEHICLE
WAIT FOR SIGNAL
WATCH FOR LOW FLYING
        AIRCRAFT
WATCH FOR PEDESTRIANS
WEIGH STATION
WINDING ROAD

YIELD
YIELD RIGHT OF WAY

Appendix N:
Penmanship Samples

Aa Bb Cc Dd Ee Ff Gg
Hh Ii Jj Kk Ll Mm Nn
Oo Pp Qq Rr Ss Tt Uu
Vv Ww Xx Yy Zz

Many adults choose to use a combination of cursive and manuscript writing.

Aa Bb Cc Dd Ee Ff Gg
Hh Ii Jj Kk Ll Mm Nn
Oo Pp Qq Rr Ss Tt Uu
Vv Ww Xx Yy Zz

Aa Bb Cc Dd Ee Ff Gg
Hh Ii Jj Kk Ll Mm Nn
Oo Pp Qq Rr Ss Tt Uu
Vv Ww Xx Yy Zz

See page 173 for guidance on using these models.

Index

J

Job. *See* Employment; Work (student's job)

Journals
Journal Writing (Strategy 58)   20, 67, 69, 155, 175, **187**, 195
Sample topics   48, 58
Uses in lesson   34, 55, 110, 171

K

Key word   140, 141
Keyboard. *See* Computers
Kinesthetic learners   19, 21, 25, 82, 153, 155
KN sound   128
KWL   108

L

Language Patterns (Strategy 12)   63, 67, 76, 86, **90**
Large-print books   22
LD. *See* Learning disabilities
LE ending   167, 213
Learner, The Adult   **13-26**
Learning disabilities   7, 24, 25, 104, 113
Learning styles   **18-25**, 82, 110, 124, 126, 171. *See also* Learning disabilities
Strategies related to   142, 147, 150, 153, 154, 155, 158
Left brain   20, 142, 171
Lesson, parts of   45, 46
Lesson planning   **43-70**
Modification   9, 37, 45, 46, 47, 52, 54, 70, 86
Samples   57, 59, 61, 63, 65, 67, 69
Steps   45, 48, 49, 54, 70
Student's role   8, 24, 25, 35, 47, 124, 148, 174, 197. *See also* Goals, student's
Tips   46, 47, 70

Let's Find Out (Strategy 16)   19, 59, 67, 69, 105, **108**
Letter reversals   24, 97, 98
Letters, writing   58, 68, 169, 171, 175, 177, 185, 188, 189, 195
Liability issues   29
Library   22, 29, 35, 47, 49, 56, 58, 77, 88
Light   21, 22, 23, 25, 31, 96
Lines of Progression (Strategy 11)   63, 86, **89**
Lists, writing   20, 171, 172, 175, 177
Literacy, defined   7
Literacy organization   9, 29, 35, 46, 49, 196, 197
LITSTART   iii, 4
Logs. *See* Journals
Long words
Defined   123
How to teach   146, 157, 167
Long Words (Strategies 44-49)   69, 138, 139, 155, **159-166**
Tutor Checks   161, 165
Tutoring strategies   159, 160, 162, 163, 164, 166
When to teach   68, 69, 109, 138
Look, Ma, No Pen! (Strategy 41)   19, 25, 67, 69, 139, **155**
LY ending   68, 152

M

Magazines
For ESL   51, 56, 57, 75, 80
For literacy   34, 50, 58
Magnifying sheets   22
Mail   31, 32, 33, 49, 50, 88, 189
Manuscript writing. *See* Printing
Mapping (Strategy 25)   19, 20, 25, 67, 69, 105, **118-119**
Mapping for writing. *See* Guided Writing (Strategies 53 and 54)

Maps   29, 30, 50, 58, 59, 78, 88, 95, 106. *See also* Guided Writing (Strategies 53 and 54); Mapping (Strategy 25)
Master Topics List   32, 33, 34, 48, 56, 58, 70
Materials
For first session   29
How to select   8, 10, 31, 35, 45, 52, 54, 197
Sources of   9, 49, 50, 51
Math   7, 20, 24, 34, 51, 60, 61, 78
Mechanical abilities   8
Medical issues   76, 88. *See also specific impairments*
Memos   185
Mental impairments   24
Mini-goals   193
Mission   5
Mistakes
Documentation   195
During assessment   37-42
How to handle   8, 10, 11, 31, 74, 76, 104, 125, 145, 174, 175, 196
Spelling   151, 178, 187
Tutor's   8, 70, 102
Money   51, 56, 61, 62, 80, 87, 88, 91
Morning person   21
Motivation   9, 11, 17, 21, 47, 55, 96, 98, 148, 196, 197. *See also* Emotions; Goals, student's
Recognizing achievement   35, 193, 195
Writing   17, 177, 186
Moving (Strategy 4)   63, **82**, 86
Muscle strength   21
Music   8, 17, 18, 20, 21, 50, 55
Myths   99, 100, 101, 172

N

Name, student's   31, 60, 61, 62, 64, 65, 77
National Institute for Literacy   9
Nervousness   29, 104

R

Read Aloud (Strategy 21)   25, 52, 59, 67, 69, 105, **114**
Reading   **93-120**
　Advanced level   53, 68, 69
　Aloud   19, 112, 113, 114
　Assessment   36, 41
　Beginning level   64, 65
　ESL   60, 61, 62, 63
　General   45, 46, 54, 95, 96, 142
　Intermediate level   53, 66, 67
Reading Exercise of Where to Start   37, 40
Reading Together (Strategy 20)   19, 20, 25, 65, 67, 105, **113**
Recipes   95, 102, 195
Recorded Spelling (Strategy 43)   19, 139, 155, **158**
Remembering (poor student retention)   11, 19, 22, 98
Reports, writing   188
Rereading   55, 114, 144
Research, tutor   3, 8, 9, 25, 90, 103
Restlessness   21
Reversals   24, 97, 98
Rewriting material. *See* Tutor Rewrite (Strategy 17)
Rhyming words. *See* Word families
Right and wrong things to say   11
Right brain   20, 153, 171
Rights for students with disabilities   24
Role playing   19, 20, 38, 54, 74, 86
　Role Playing (Strategy 13)   57, 63, 86, 88, **91**
Routine, developing a   45, 47
Rules, handling exceptions   8

S

Salt   155
Same and Different (Strategy 23)   19, 20, 67, 69, 105, **116**
Sand   155
Sandpaper   155
School
　As tutoring site   29
　Student's   7, 15, 16, 32, 88, 189
　Student's children   33, 50, 91, 185

Schwa   212, 213, 214, 215, 216
Science   5, 34, 49, 78, 95
Scrabble   155
Seating   9, 21, 22, 30
Self-image   17
Sensitivity to light   23, 25
Sentences, Dictated (Strategy 55)   **184**
SH sound   128, 130, 131, 135, 136, 207
Sight words   111, 124, 139, **147**, 264, 265
　Advanced level   68, 69, 265
　Beginning level   64, 65, 66, 67, 264
　ESL   60, 61, 62, 63
　Intermediate level   66, 67, 68, 69, 264
　When to teach   19, 25, 123
Signs   10, 50, 195, 266, 268
SION ending   68, 128, 214
Site for tutoring   29, 35
Skills Checklists   54, 60, 62, 64, 66, 68
Skipping material   10, 11, 114, 148
Slang. *See* Grammar: errors
Slash marks   126
Smoking   21
Snacks   21, 196
Social studies   34, 49, 78, 95
Soft C and G   127, 128, 135, 146, 164
Sound It Out (Strategy 28)   19, 25, 67, 132, 139, **142**, 155
Speaking English   **71-92**. *See also* ESL
Spelling
　Aloud   19
　As a goal   15, 32, 193, 195
　Assessment   36, 195
　General   123, 172, 184
　How to teach   150-158, 175, 178, 189
　Learning styles   20, 155
　Mistakes   11, 19, 24, 171, 172, 175
　Rules   136, 137, 152
　Temporary. *See* Temporary spelling
　When to teach   10, 55, 66, 68, 142

Spelling Patterns 1 (Strategy 37)   19, 59, 65, 67, 139, **151**, 155
Spelling Patterns 2 (Strategy 38)   19, 67, 69, 136, 139, **152**, 155
Spelling Prep (Strategy 36)   19, 65, 67, 139, **150**, 155
Spelling Tricks (Strategy 42)   67, 69, 139, 155, **156-157**
Sports   15, 17, 19, 50
Squinting   22
Story Outline (Strategy 24)   19, 20, 67, 69, 105, **117**
Strategies
　How to select   9, 47, 54, 61-70, 105, 125, 139, 193, 196
　Reading   106-119
　Speaking   79-91
　Word Study   140-166
　Writing   176-189
Stress   25, 98
Students, sample   6, 16, 48, 56, 58. *See also* Lesson planning - Samples
Success. *See* Celebrating success
Suffixes   66, 68, 130, 136, 137, 143, 152
Syllables   19, 114, 136, 138, 143, 152, 157, 162. *See also* Long words
Symbols, learning   60, 61

T

Tactile learners   19, 25, 155
Tape recorders   19, 24, 50, 55, 112, 158, 195
Telephone   29, 50, 56
Television   32, 50, 195
　ESL   55, 61, 63, 78
Temperature   21, 31, 96
Temporary spelling
　Samples   172, 176, 179, 188
　Temporary Spelling (Strategy 50)   19, 20, 66, 68, 155, 175, **176**
　Uses   178, 188, 189
Terminology, using   89, 125
Testing, formal   52, 193, 195